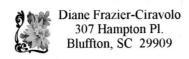

The Great Sea Island Storm of 1893

BY BILL AND FRAN MARSCHER

MERCER UNIVERSITY PRESS | 2003 | MACON, GEORGIA

The Great
Sea Island Storm
of 1893

ISBN 0-86554-867-6
MUP/P249

© 2004 Mercer University Press
1400 Coleman Avenue
Macon, Georgia 31207

First Edition.

Book design by Burt & Burt Studio.

∞The paper used in this publication meets the minimum requirements
of American National Standard for Information Sciences—Permanence of Paper
for Printed Library Materials, ANSI Z39.48-1992.

Library of Congress Cataloging-in-Publication Data

Marscher, Bill, 1929-
The great sea island storm of 1893 / by Bill and Fran Marscher.—1st ed.
p. cm.
Includes bibliographical references (p.   ).
ISBN 0-86554-867-6 (pbk. : alk. paper)
1. Hurricanes—South Carolina—History—19th century.
2. Hurricanes—Georgia—History—19th century. 3. Gullahs--South Carolina.
I. Marscher, Fran. II. Title.

QC945.M37 2004
975.7'99041—dc22

2004000675

Contents

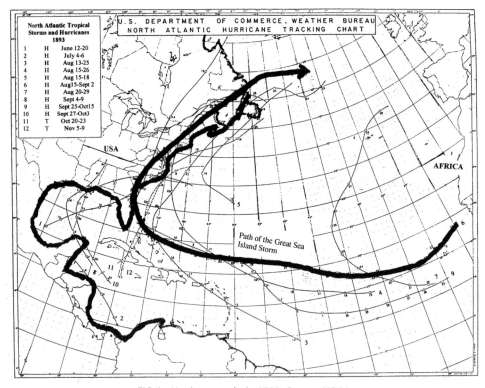

North Atlantic Tropical Storms and Hurricanes 1893

1	H	June 12-20
2	H	July 4-6
3	H	Aug 13-25
4	H	Aug 15-26
5	H	Aug 15-18
6	H	Aug15-Sept 2
7	H	Aug 20-29
8	H	Sept 4-9
9	H	Sept 25-Oct15
10	H	Sept 27-Oct3
11	T	Oct 20-23
12	T	Nov 5-9

U.S. DEPARTMENT OF COMMERCE, WEATHER BUREAU
NORTH ATLANTIC HURRICANE TRACKING CHART

USA

AFRICA

Path of the Great Sea Island Storm

FIG 1. Hurricane tracks in 1893, Source: NOAA

Preface

The Great Sea Island Storm of 1893 is a heartbreaking tale. As many as 2,000 people, maybe more, were killed in the hurricane that hit coastal Georgia and walloped South Carolina with winds up to 120 miles per hour and a ten- to twelve-foot storm surge. Another 1,000 may have died afterward from injury, dehydration, starvation, and illness. So long and arduous was the process of restoring life's basic necessities, the storm's victims—mostly former slaves and their descendants—came to be called the "storm sufferers."

Although a period of scientific and technological advances preceded the Great Sea Island Storm, hurricanes were still mysterious monsters from the sea at the end of the nineteenth century. Americans simply did not know what to expect from them. Those living in the rural areas and on the remote coastal islands had no way of getting even tentative warnings ahead of time to try to flee from a hurricane—or to try to batten down against it.

The destructive hurricane of August 1893 demonstrated to the nation that these storms, called "cyclones" at the time, were killers on land as well as at sea. It sent a signal to the nation to start paying attention to them—in order to protect citizens in their homes as well as ships and their crews. It provided Clara Barton of the American Red Cross with her first experience in hurricane relief and recovery. Grimly, this event showed the nation for the first time that hurricane catastrophes leave a lot of misery and chaos in their wake, long after the winds die down.

We two coastal South Carolinians have been intrigued by this great hurricane for many years. Growing up in Beaufort, South

Carolina, Bill was a young boy when he discovered old newspaper clippings about it. He began to ask questions and listen to his family's stories. Living on the second floor of a waterfront warehouse in Beaufort, his grandparents escaped injury and possible death by wading in the rising, thrashing waters around their home the night the ocean charged ashore.

Gradually, Bill collected photographs and copies of diaries and journals and correspondence from others who had survived the night of the storm. He followed up with research in the Library of Congress, the American Red Cross headquarters, the US Weather Service, and other sources. He consulted with modern-day meteorologists. He gathered more stories and more data—not only about the storm itself but also about the long, arduous aftermath—and about hurricanes in general.

In the late 1990s, we began the sorting and organizing and assembling of the material—to write a book. There was a whale of a story there—and there was more. There was the terrifying example of hurricane impacts on individuals, on landscapes, on the economy, and on whole societies. The more we learned about hurricanes, the keener we felt *today's* potential for catastrophe again in the communities struck hardest by the Great Sea Island Storm. Nearly 1,000,000 people now live in the coastal strip that proved to be such a dangerous location in 1893.

Beaufort County, which took the brunt the Great Sea Island Storm, is the home of 27,000-acre Hilton Head Island, now internationally famous as a posh golf-resort community. It is the home of the historic city of Beaufort, frequently identified as one of the nation's "most livable small towns." It is the home of St. Helena Island, well known for preserving and promoting the Gullah culture, and of Parris Island, the unforgettable US Marine Corps training depot.

One expert estimates that a hurricane today with the intensity and the path of the August 1893 hurricane would wreck more than $32 billion in insured property as it slammed ashore and then traveled through the eastern third of the United States. Whether the coastal residents and vacationers would escape with their lives would depend largely on whether they could—and would—evacuate in time to miss the storm surge.

Just as our research forced us to look at the predicament of the people now living in the demolition zone of the Great Sea Island Storm, it forced us to look at similar potential disaster areas in the coastal zones from Maine to Texas. In the twentieth century, the numbers of hurricane deaths dramatically declined while the value of hurricane damage dramatically increased. Early in the twenty-first century, however, growth in populations and growth in investments in the hurricane-prone property along the shorelines of the Atlantic and Gulf of Mexico represent a startling trend. As the coastal regions lead the nation in the tourism, retirement, and real estate industries, the nation's hurricane experts predict more and more costly property losses and fear a rise in the numbers of hurricane fatalities.

As it turns out, we have written not one book but two. Our first book, *Living in the Danger Zone*, describes hurricane risks and potential disaster scenes in the nation's hurricane-vulnerable areas—along with potential remedies. *The Great Sea Island Storm of 1893* describes hurricane devastation and its sorrowful aftermath at one time in one vulnerable place—the place that is our home.

Bill and Fran Marscher
Beaufort County, South Carolina

FIG 2.
Charleston, South Carolina, to Savannah, Georgia coast, showing the path of the Great Sea Island Storm, Source: Harpers Magazine 1894

CHAPTER 1

Life in the Lowcountry Long Ago

To learn and labor truly to get mine own living, and to do my
duty in that state of life, unto which it shall please God to call me.
BOOK OF COMMON PRAYER

In 1893, about 200,000 people, 50,000 of European origin and 150,000 of African origin, lived in what is called the South Carolina Lowcountry, the Charleston area and the coastal region south of it. In the Lowcountry's southern tip, Beaufort County— called the "black county"—blacks outnumbered whites ten to one.[1] Whites called the blacks "Negroes" or, locally, "Gullahs." The blacks called themselves "we." They spoke a lilting language also called "Gullah," an English dialect flavored with African rhythms, words and speech patterns. Whites who communicated often with the Gullahs could understand their language, and some could speak it. Those who heard Gullah only occasionally were at a loss.

---

[1] David Duncan Wallace, *South Carolina: A Short History* (Columbia: University of South Carolina Press, 1951) 711.

With the Civil War, locally called "de big gun shoot," the Gullahs had been granted freedom from slavery. With the gigantic hurricane thirty years later, called "de big blow," the Gullahs were dealt a blow that proved to be another life-changing milestone.

The Lay of the Land. A transitional zone between the continent and the ocean, the Lowcountry is flat and low, with nothing on it to stop a storm surge—that mound of water that washes ashore along with a hurricane. Interlaced with creeks, rivers, sounds, salt marsh, and freshwater swampland, the land in the Lowcountry that is high and dry enough to be suitable for human habitation comprises less than half the total area.

In the estuaries' winding water paths, the tide rises and falls six to nine feet twice a day, constantly changing the vistas. Salt marsh, thousands of acres of it shifting colors during the seasons from brown to green to golden and brown again, sways almost constantly in the breeze. The "pluff" mud on the creek banks, as soft as pudding, as black as ink and alive with the tiny creatures that feed the larger creatures of the estuaries, emits an earthy scent. On the edges of the tidal waters, palmettos' crisp fronds rattle with the movement of tree life, and moss-draped live oaks twist and then hold their huge arms in every direction toward the sunlight.

Beaufort County consists of a series of peninsulas and islands, including the barrier islands; the larger of the inhabited islands, called the "Sea Islands." Many of the "no-name" islands are nothing more than small piles of sand held tentatively together by sparse, scrubby vegetation. In the late nineteenth century, the island-dwelling Gullahs lived in little frame houses as fragile as the islands themselves. Few of their windows had panes. More had simple wooden shutters, flung open in the hopes of catching a breeze in the summer, and latched tight in hopes of keeping out the wind in the winter. Roofs were made of rough-hewn native wood shingles, chimneys of worn bricks. Many floors were packed sand. The bright blue paint adorning the trim on a lot of the houses demonstrated a lingering superstition that such color would ward off evil spirits.

The islands' earth drained poorly and supported mosquitoes and diseases, including the dreaded malaria and yellow fever. The islands' lands were known to erode, and known also to experience periodic attacks by the dreaded cyclones.

On the islands' sandy two-rutted roads, the people traveled by foot, by horse, or by two-wheel ox cart. To go to the mainland or to other islands, they had two choices. They could row their small, flat-bottomed boats, called "bateaux," working their big, handmade oars in steady rhythms over long distances through small creeks and open sounds; or they could row out to meet the regular steamers that traveled in the deep waterways between Charleston and Savannah.

The diet of these island dwellers depended on the season, the luck of the weather, the tides and the energy and skill put into farming and fishing. Fish, shrimp, oysters, mussels, clams, and Atlantic blue crabs were plentiful. Plowing with oxen and small-boned, wiry horses called "marsh tackies," the Gullahs worked the earth to get out of it what food they could for themselves and their animals. Unfortunately, the sandy soil was not especially productive in those years, having been depleted of its nutrients by a century of raising cotton.

Although the coastal dwellers ate a lot of turnip greens and turnip roots, they depended on corn most of all. They ate corn, grits, and cornmeal. They fed corn to their horses, chickens, oxen, and cows, and corn shucks to their pigs. The late summer crop of feed corn and the early fall crop of sweet potatoes served as their winter staples.

For cash, islanders planted a few rows of cotton to pick in late summer and early fall. No longer "king," however, cotton was not selling for its pre-Civil War prices. Times were different, the soil was poorer from years of cultivation, the seed stock had deteriorated, and the cotton was of less quality. One year's cotton harvest produced hardly enough money to pay taxes on the land.

The Civil War's Legacy. As a practical matter, the Union troops' capture of Beaufort County in 1861 had ended slavery on the cotton plantations of the Sea Islands. Then President Abraham Lincoln ended it legally across the South by issuing the Emancipation Proclamation effective January 1, 1863. During the Reconstruction Era of 1865–1874, thousands of Gullahs bought or were given small tracts out of plantations they had previously worked as slaves. General Tecumseh Sherman's Special Field Order No. 15 in 1865 set aside "the islands from Charleston, south, and the abandoned rice fields along the rivers for 30 miles back from the sea, to the country bordering St. John's River, Florida for the freedmen."[2]

For a time, the island freedmen shared political power with their black brethren on the mainland. In the years immediately after the Civil War, what had been the state of South Carolina was "Military District No. 2." All whites in any way connected to the Confederacy were treated as traitors and disenfranchised. By the thousands, black men registered to vote. They took over local and state governments and elected the state's first black congressman, Robert Smalls of Beaufort.

---

[2]Virginia C. Holmgren, *Hilton Head: A Sea Island Chronicle* (Hilton Head Island SC: Hilton Head Island Publishing Co., 1959) 109.

FIG 3. The way it was on St. Helena Island, Source: Penn Center

The Sea Island Gullahs had the unique advantage of special schools established during the war. Shortly after Union troops set up headquarters on Hilton Head Island, missionaries from Massachusetts, Pennsylvania and New York had come to the islands to teach practical life skills, reading, writing, history, science, music, and art. Later, the town fathers of Hilton Head Island's Mitchelville, the first municipality of freedmen, passed the first compulsory education law in America. Although most of those schools for the children of the recently freed slaves did not endure, for a couple of years they served a population that otherwise would have had no chance of getting a formal education. The schools helped the Sea Island families establish a tradition that included education for children as an important part of community life.

And yet, as the freed slaves took charge of their own lives and their communities, they had to scramble to make a living for their families in the last quarter of the nineteenth century. Just as the South began timidly to recover from the war one small, sandy cotton field and noisy textile mill at a time, the United States became part of a worldwide depression. Any meager investments that came into the South in those decades did not trickle into the economy of these islands.

Although island residents "caught the boat" to come to town once in a while, their stay was usually only long enough to pay their pittances of taxes, to deliver whatever they had to sell and to buy a pair of shoes or a sewing needle. Institutions on the mainland that might have broadened the horizons and enriched the lives of the free, land-owning Gullahs were far away. South Carolina's Sea Islanders in 1893 were in locations too remote to benefit from the telegraph and the railroad—modern systems beginning to serve the rest of the nation.

The Gullahs' obvious disadvantages included their isolation, their history as an enslaved people, and the poverty of the region. Then came election in 1890 of "Pitchfork" Ben Tillman as South Carolina's governor. By 1893, Tillman had arranged for the Upstate's representation to increase in state government, for the majority black Lowcountry to lose representation, and for the Negroes to be systematically discouraged from voting altogether.

Still, in a subtropical climate, lush with live oaks and palmettos and magnolias, with seafood plentiful and free, with freedom theirs for three decades, these Gullahs in 1893 lived better lives than they or their parents and grandparents had lived before "de big gun shoot." A whole new generation had come into adulthood since the end of the Civil War.

As physically demanding as their way of life was, before the hurricane, these farming and fishing families did not necessarily think of themselves as victims of their circumstances. The words of W. E. B. DuBois, the Harvard-educated black sociologist of the early twentieth century, gave his version of their philosophy: "The black tropical worker looked upon work as a necessary evil and maintained his right to balance the relative allurements of leisure and satisfaction at any particular day, hour, or season…White labor brought to America the habit of regular, continual toil, which he regarded as a great moral duty. Black labor brought the idea of toil as a necessary evil, ministering to the pleasures of life."[3]

True, the Gullahs on these remote islands of the South Carolina wrestled with the elements for their daily bread, but they did not have to hustle their wares among strangers on hard, cold, city pavement. Their modest dwellings were on mostly sandy, low lands, but

---

[3]Asa Gordon, *Sketches of Negro Life and History in South Carolina* (Columbia: University of South Carolina Press, 1929) 11.

FIG 4. Richard Middleton and his bateau on St. Helena Island, Source: Penn Center

they owned their homes and the land under them. They had great blue herons and abundant wildlife to watch. Spring came early to the islands. They had the creeks and the woods and the fields and one another—and they had freedom. They sang together and helped one another make it through the hard times. In their small praise houses, they enjoyed a regular "shout," a lively, communal dance that lasted into the night.

Uncomplicated Commerce. Although prosperity was almost nowhere to be found in the South between the end of the Civil War and the end of the nineteenth century, the whites in general fared better physically and financially than the blacks. Most of the wealthy, white antebellum planters' families had fled Beaufort County when the Yankees took over in 1861, and most never returned. Thirty years later, those who had come back were eking out a living, just as the blacks were eking out a living. And yet, the whites' experience of having others work for them in the past set a pattern for hiring farm workers rather than trying to hoe every cotton row themselves. By using others to do much of the manual labor, a few were thus able to produce a little surplus.

White "carpetbaggers" from the North and recent European immigrants also had moved to South Carolina's coast. For the most part, they settled on the highest grounds in the region, not on the remote islands. In addition to farming and fishing, this group became the merchants, bankers, doctors, and lawyers of what they hoped one day would be a growing region filled with opportunity. Some of the more industrious could spend money on their homes, eat meat several times a week, buy brandy occasionally, and coffee. Some could afford to send their children off to private boarding schools in the North.

In Charleston and Savannah, on the great wharves jutting out into the rivers, cotton, rice, turpentine, and lumber were loaded onto ships; manufactured goods came in—shoes and belts, clothing, felt hats, furniture, books, oil, steel tools. Within these trade centers of the Lowcountry flowed almost enough money to keep going, in one way or another, many of the churches, galleries, museums, theaters, and courthouses that had been built from the wealth of indigo, rice, and cotton and had survived the Civil War.

A few Lowcountry residents owned pleasure sailing yachts. They traveled by horse and buggy, train, and steamer—and hired black oarsmen to row bateaux for them. They enjoyed the luxury of being able to race their horses and boats instead of using them only for plowing and hauling crops to market. Some hunted wild turkeys, quail, doves, and deer in the woodlands and fished for drumfish in the sounds in the spring—for pleasure, as well as for food.

A sample from the listings in the city assessor's report from the *Yearbook, City of Charleston, SC 1893*, reveals the nature of personal wealth in that community: 1,545 horses and mules, worth $118,435; gold and silver watches and plate, valued at $66,527; 466 piano fortes, melodeons and cabinet organs, valued at $38,405. The assessed value of real estate and personal property in Charleston was $23.7 million—about $450 million in today's dollars.

Even Beaufort, the small town on Port Royal Island between Charleston and Savannah, had some fine antebellum houses, a bathing salon, and a shaving salon. It also had a little theater and a French millinery shop.

In addition to the enterprises linked to the ports, a few other wage-earning jobs existed in the region. Near the mouths of the rivers, health-care professionals tested, treated, fed, and provided

lodging for immigrants for weeks at a time in the "quarantine stations." Government lighthouses and other public work provided
small but dependable salaries for a few families. Oyster factories
were beginning to give young, able men and women a way to con-
vert a ready natural resource into a few bucks. Oyster gatherers
harvested from the creek banks, shuckers broke open the shells, and
fire tenders threw the logs to keep the boilers for steaming and can-
ning going brightly.

The Lowcountry's only real industry with substantial payroll,
though, was phosphate mining. Farmers in this country and in
Europe had learned that certain rocks, in addition to organic
manure, could provide essential nutrients to their over-cultivated
crop soils. Chunks of phosphate that could be converted into fertil-
izer were readily accessible in the riverbeds of the coastal region.
Miners had begun to dredge and dig in South Carolina's navigable
waterways in 1870. Over the next couple of decades, the tonnage
extracted and exported from the waters grew quickly to almost
250,000 tons annually.[4]

By the mid-1880s, those who had invested in the mining enterprises were beginning to make profits. They had attracted other
entrepreneurs and generated welcome commercial activity in northern Beaufort County. By the time of the Great Sea Island Storm, the
companies were employing as many as 3,000 people and sending
the state one dollar per ton, providing important revenue. Such an
industry was an important boon for poor, rural South Carolina.[5]

---

[4]Philip E. Chazal, *A Sketch of the South Carolina Phosphate Industry* (Charleston SC: Lucas-Richardson Lithography and Printing Co., 1904) 70.

[5]"South Carolina in 1888," *News and Courier* (Charleston SC), Pamphlet, 13.

On August 25, 1893, the mining plants [fleet] of the various [Beaufort County] companies consisted of twelve dredges, eleven wash boats, ten tug boats, one hundred and six lighters [flat barges] and ninety-five tonging flats.

Coosaw River was…alive with the huge dredging machines, wash boats and numbers of lighters and small craft. The numerous tug boats flitting to and fro, the shrill scream of whistles, the clank of chains as the huge dippers were lowered to the bottom and raised with their load of phosphate rock, the sullen roar of the *John Kennedy* [a gigantic dredge] as the mighty endless chain revolved with its thirty-six ponderous dippers weighing more than a ton each—the whole presented a picture of active industry never to be forgotten…."[6]

Freedom had come, indeed, to the Lowcountry, and cash had begun to find its way into a few hands, but neither the freedom nor the few dollars had prepared the Lowcountry residents—the former slaves, the whites, the newcomers, the landowners, the tenant farmers, even the richest men in one of the country's most poverty-stricken regions—for the Great Sea Island Storm.

Ambushed by the Hurricane. The big blow to the South Carolina Sea Islands and lowlands came when the South's political and moral condition was only slightly better than its condition as a war zone thirty years earlier. In much of South Carolina, ill will, brutality, and near-anarchy ran rampant between the races, and the Ku Klux Klan was riding high, wreaking its terrorism and influence openly and secretly. The hostility and violence the Klan exhibited did not manifest itself in Beaufort, "the black county," at that time. And yet, a

---

[6]South Carolina General Assembly, Board of Phosphate Commission, *Third Annual Report to the General Assembly of the State of South Carolina at the Regular Session of 1893* (Columbia SC: Charles A. Calvo Jr., 1893) 14.

letter published in Beaufort's white-owned *Palmetto Post* in 1890 explained in detail why the writer believed the lynching of eight Negroes in nearby Barnwell County a few months earlier had been absolutely justifiable as a "necessity."

One historian described the South Carolina situation as perpetual political and psychological combat—small farmers against planters, poor against rich, new against old, white against black.[7] Another described class antagonism as the overwhelming force in South Carolina politics in the 1890s.[8]

The killer hurricane, another "strong force," hit the state's coast in the worst possible place—the flat, remote Sea Islands. It hit at the worst possible time—near the end of harvest season, on high tide. Its violence was most ruthless against the nation's most vulnerable citizens—former slaves and their offspring, the Gullahs.

[7]Mary C. Simms Oliphant, *The History of South Carolina* (River Forest IL/ Summit NJ/ Palo Alto CA/ Dallas TX/ Atlanta GA: Laidlaw Bros., 1964) 295.

[8]Walter Edgar, *South Carolina A History* (Columbia: University of South Carolina Press, 1998) 437.

CHAPTER 2

As "Dirty Weather" Gathered

The wind bloweth where it listeth, and thou hearest the sound
thereof, but canst not tell whence it cometh, and whither it goeth.
JOHN 3:8, KJV

I n 1890, when Weather Bureau "forecast official" Lewis N. Jesunofsky came to Charleston as the South Carolina Lowcountry's new observer, he saw one of his responsibilities as the community's safety from weather trauma.[9] Yet he would have no way of knowing or predicting the path and intensity of the hurricane that would come ashore August 27, 1893. Even if Mr. Jesunofsky had realized that extreme calamity was on its way, he had only a marginal warning system in place, and he had no way to get word to the tens of thousands of people living on the islands between Savannah and Charleston when they were in danger.

---

[9]Laylon Wayne Jordan with Robert Duke, Jr. and Ted Rosengarten, *A History of Storms on the South Carolina Coast* (Charleston: South Carolina Sea Grant Consortium, 1983) 88.

Using ships' logs, meteorologists later traced the Great Sea Island Storm backward to the tropical seas near the Cape Verde Islands off the coast of Africa. They deduced that it began building its force in that area about August 15. Not until the twenty-second, from ships that had come into port, did coastal weather officials learn of its existence. Marine reports by that time showed low pressure and high winds, evidence of the swirling and pumping of an embryonic, vigorous system.

Not until the afternoon of Friday, August 25, when heavy waves of the expanded hurricane began to beat against the beaches, did news of the oncoming weather system begin to trickle out to some of those who lived along the coast.

Little warning. Although Georgia and South Carolina's Lowcountry residents might have heard the surfs' loud, rhythmical pounding on the beaches, it is probable that none of them ever saw the big swells signifying that a major hurricane was churning offshore. Those who lived on the islands in those days lived on the highest ground available, usually well inland from the ocean.

On the basis of ships' reports and information telegraphed from Washington, the Weather Bureaus in Charleston, Savannah, and Wilmington began flying storm signals (red banners) from official rooftops and posting bulletins on street corners in their cities. Perhaps they also mailed a few postcards to warn local residents. They predicted northeast gales, with rain, for Saturday, August 26. When the strong winds and rain did not show up as forecast, Charleston's Mr. Jesunofsky apologized to the public, conceding that the "warnings were somewhat premature."

Actually, the hurricane was still on the way, about to send the "highest tide known" into St. Augustine, Florida "in waves eight feet high" early Sunday morning. Neighboring Jacksonville, however, caught "only a good stiff breeze as compared with Savannah's."[10]

On Saturday in Savannah, readers of *The Morning News* could learn about the storm by looking at the *bottom* of page eight: The small headline said, "Another Storm Coming." Under that was this additional information: "It Is Centered Off Florida, and Is Said to Be Moving Northwest." A special bulletin issued Saturday afternoon in Savannah had a bit more detail: "High winds prevailed in the Bahamas all night Friday…. Northeasterly gales and general rains are indicated for Saturday night and Sunday on the coast of the south Atlantic states, including the west coast of the Florida Peninsula."

The News and Courier of Charleston likewise treated the coming hurricane as little more than minor weather news. Under a Saturday headline saying "Synopsis of Weather," was this sentence: "The area of minimum pressure (or cyclone) east of Florida is moving northwestward and is apparently located over south Florida, where the tides are high and northeast winds are reported."

To Norfolk, Boston, New York, Baltimore, and Philadelphia, the word went out from the Weather Bureau that the storm "existing off the coast" rendered it unsafe for vessels to leave port for the South until further notice. Dangerous gales were expected during the next forty-eight hours.

Savannah's *Sunday Morning News* reported the following on page eight: "What the present cyclone now coming up the Florida coast will do remains to be seen. It is coming very slowly, but it is predicted that it will strike here this morning. The…cyclone comes from the Gulf Stream east of the Florida coast. Yesterday morning it

---

[10] "At St. Augustine Waves Eight Feet High Break upon the City," *Morning News* (Savannah GA), August 29, 1893, 4.

had advanced somewhat nearer to the coast with its center east of the Florida coast." The article continued, "At its present rate of progress, the storm center will pass Savannah early this morning, causing northeast gales along the Georgia coast."

The newspapers said nothing about the likelihood of coastal residents being subjected to one of the planet's most dangerous weather phenomena. They told nothing of when and where the hurricane's highest winds and storm surge might strike land. They recommended nothing to their readers about boarding up, moving boats, protecting the livestock, and getting out of the way. They had no way of knowing what we now call the eye would pass directly through Savannah.

Sunday at noon the official Savannah observers sent special dispatches to President Benjamin Harrison and on to the New England coast, alerting them to expect dangerous gales. The eye of the hurricane traveled east of Jacksonville, Florida, at about 5 P.M.; through Savannah, Georgia, at about 10 P.M. Savannah Weather Bureau Observer Smyth reported what he called the lowest barometric reading ever recorded in the United States, 28.31 inches; winds of 70 miles per hour; 5.17 inches of rainfall before midnight Sunday and 5.04 inches of rainfall after midnight.

By 6 A.M. Monday the eye was slightly west of Augusta, Georgia.

Hardest hit. For the coastal dwellers, Sunday night was a night of sheer terror. Those who lived through it never forgot it. The roughest violence struck those caught in the hurricane's right forward quadrant, the residents of coastal South Carolina.

Charleston's Weather Bureau officially described the event afterward:

[There was a] 10-foot storm-wave along the lower sea-coast islands, and a 5 1/2-foot storm-wave in and around Charleston.

When it is borne in mind that two direct forces act upon the water at the same time, it may not surprise the most skeptical mind. On the outer edges of the storm-center there is a powerful downward and up-curving air-pressure; this, in conjunction with the spiral and rapid inward flowing winds, produces such an immense wall of water, with violent agitations on its surface, as to leave little or nothing but the solid mason-work standing.

One of the official observers wrote later: Concerning the height of ocean storm-waves, it is estimated that those of the South Atlantic frequently reach a height of 30 feet, with a breadth of 600 feet from crest to crest. Assuming, therefore, the height of ocean-waves to be 30 feet in deep water, and taking into consideration the disturbance of the surface water upon the sea islands during the storm, it would seem that at least thirteen feet of water covered that section.[11]

Charleston's weather observers began to record falling barometer readings at eleven o'clock Sunday morning. The mercury dropped to 29.076 inches before it finally began rising at about 2 A.M. Monday. The 1885 hurricane had blown the wind-velocity devices away but in 1893, having been secured thoroughly, they remained intact and recorded the enormous wind power as it attacked the city: from the northeast at 28 miles per hour at 5 A.M. Sunday; at 12:35 P.M., from the northeast but blowing 48 mph; at 8:10 P.M., from the east at 74 mph. Around midnight it dropped to 68 mph, still from the east. Monday morning, at 12:40 A.M., the wind from the east was 88 mph. Ten minutes later, the equipment

---

[11] *Year Book, City of Charleston, 1893* (Charleston SC: Walker, Evans and Cogswell Co., n.d. 268.

recorded 96-mph winds for one solid minute. At 12.50, the wind blew 120 mph in Charleston, and the scientists wrote double exclamation points after that data.

The winds dropped to 88 mph and had shifted to the southeast by 3:20 A.M., then came from the south at 66 mph by 9:16 A.M. Monday. The city had been under siege by at least gale-force winds (40 mph or more) for more than twenty-four hours and by hurricane-force winds (74 mph or more) for at least three hours of that twenty-four-hour period.[12]

More damage inland. Once the hurricane hit land, it did not break up quite as expected. By mid-afternoon on Monday, it was tearing up communities a few miles northwest of Charlotte, North Carolina. Fairly intact, it passed along the Appalachians during the night. Telegrams went to Atlantic City, New Brunswick, Philadelphia, New York, New Haven, and New London, recommending that the postmasters in those communities and in any other of the northern coastal areas be notified of pending "severe easterly gales," heavy rains and unusually high tides. On receipt of these telegrams, some newspapers issued extra editions to try to warn the public.

By 8 P.M. Monday, northeast winds were pounding West Virginia, western Pennsylvania, western New York and northwestern Ohio, while southeast winds beat on North Carolina, Virginia and Washington. A downpour of rain hit the entire region. For twenty-four hours, foul weather reigned from the Carolina shores to the western edge of Lake Erie.

With telegraph lines severed in all directions Monday night, the nation's weather map at 8 A.M. Tuesday was practically blank.

---

[12]Ibid., 269.

Subsequent reports show that the eye of the hurricane had traveled 450 miles in twelve hours, all the way to Oswego, New York. It shortly became obvious that this was no longer a symmetrical revolving hurricane but had become two, or possible three, systems, each "striving to set up its own independent whirl."[13]

By 8 P.M. Tuesday, the storm's center was a little east of Quebec, By 8 A.M. Wednesday, it was near the mouth of the Saint Lawrence River. As officially reported, the "cyclone" had traveled 3,300 miles in eight days at an average speed of 17.2 mph.[14] In today's classification system, based on wind velocities and barometric pressure—in which a Category 1 hurricane is the least intense and a Category 5 is the most intense—the Great Sea Island Storm would have been a Category 3 when it hit land.

And it was huge. The evidence is in the widespread damage reports, and in the 120-mph winds recorded in Charleston, about seventy-five miles from the eye. (Typically, the region of maximum winds prevails in a band a few miles wide surrounding the eye, which typically has a diameter of ten to twenty-five miles.) More evidence of the Great Sea Island Storm's enormity includes the length of time it took to travel through the coastal region. Such intense, sustained winds help account for the near-total destruction of many properties.

Although its winds subsided as it traveled over land, on Tuesday morning they bludgeoned Philadelphia at 48 mph and New York City at 54 mph. The storm surge was the big killer, but heavy rains created dangerous local flooding in a region that stretched from Toledo, Ohio to Baltimore, Maryland.

[13]National Weather Bureau, *Monthly Weather Review,* 21/8, August 1893.
[14]*Year Book, City of Charleston, 1893,* 248.

An unforgettable night. For the coastal dwellers of Georgia and South Carolina, Sunday night was a night of sheer terror. Those who lived through it never forgot it. What they were doing as the raging hurricane aimed for them on Sunday, August 27, 1893, comes to us now in snatches of time-weathered diaries, letters and newspaper clippings.

Some of the old-timers had encountered hurricanes before— one in 1854 and another in 1881. Some of them probably felt anxious as they observed the erratic squalls that pecked at the region as the hurricane moved toward them. Still, it is doubtful that many expected much more damage than the downing of a few rotten water oaks and a bit of erosion on the region's soft shorelines. As the hurricane chugged toward them, the coastal folk stayed where they were and continued to do what they had been doing. Mostly, on that warm Sunday of August 27, they were hoping to relax and have fun.

On the beach at Tybee Island at the mouth of the Savannah River, a large group from Augusta, Georgia had been enjoying a pleasure outing, popularly called an "excursion." Having taken the train to Tybee, they had no way to get back except over the railroad track—sections of it already blown over with sand by mid-afternoon. From the rattling train they could see the flooding tide within three feet of the Lazaretto Creek bridge, rising three feet per hour. Despite the treacherous conditions, these "excursionists" all were brought back safely to the mainland. That was not the case for those who tried to leave later.[15]

The quarantine stations in the mouths of the harbors, some of the most storm-exposed facilities in the region, took beatings early

---

[15]"Almost a Wreck," *Morning News,* August 29, 1893, 1.

in the day. By Sunday afternoon, barks from Norway, Great Britain, and Italy, moored on a quarantine wharf in the Savannah River, had been dashed into the marsh. Before the telephone lines went out at quarantine headquarters, the doctor there reported that his house was "shaking like a leaf and water was pouring in through the roof." In the city of Savannah itself, tin roofs, smoke stacks, electric wires, and awnings were flying through the city by late afternoon.[16]

In Beaufort, according to Senator W. J. Verdier, "The fearful storm…started Saturday evening with a light rain. It kept up Sunday morning, but not heavy enough to keep churchgoers away from morning services. The wind began to rise at about three o'clock, and it was not long before it attained a velocity of forty miles an hour. "It was not long before trees began to be uprooted and scattered 'helter skelter.'"[17]

A few weeks after the hurricane, Rachel Mather, headmistress of Beaufort's Mather Industrial School for black female students, recorded her recollections of the harbingers of the horrors of Sunday night: "On that sad Sabbath, never to be forgotten, when a thousand men, women, and children looked out on sea and shore for the last time, the pitying heavens put on a pall of sack-cloth and early in the morning brooded in silence over the doomed islands. Ere noon the wind wailed piteously and the Bay moaned ominously as if aware of the death and destruction they were bringing in, as if conscious of the pain and woe they were about to inflict on man and beast."[18]

---

[16]"Mad Ruin of the Winds Savannah Swept by Terrible Hurricane," *Morning News,* August 28, 1893, n.p.

[17]"Senator Verdier's Story of the Storm," *News and Courier* (Charleston SC), September 3, 1893, 2.

[18]R. C. Mather, *The Storm Swept Coast of South Carolina,* 1894, **n.p.**, Historical Collection, Beaufort South Carolina County Library.

Dreaded storm signals. Along with the swampy Savannah River lowlands, various island settlements—on Hilton Head Island, Daufuskie Island, St. Helena Island, Lady's Island, Edisto Island, Kiawah Island, Folly Island, Sullivan's Island, and Isle of Palms—lay a boat trip away from the cities of Charleston and Savannah. On Saturday before the disaster, only in those cities could anyone see the storm flags fluttering from the rooftop of the Agriculture Department's Weather Bureau offices or read the small, brief warning bulletins posted around town.

In Charleston, former mayor William A. Courtenay said the city "held its breath" when the dreaded storm signals were hoisted. He referred to a "heavy northeast gale" Saturday night and added, "It was hoped the city would not fall within the track of the cyclone." Alas, on Sunday, the weather was "exceedingly dirty." The wind rose again in "fitful, angry gusts." Out of the northeast, a "muddy twinge" suggested plenty of rain and wind to come. A "heavy mist thickened to a wall of cloud, and there was no doubt the dreaded cyclone was on the way."

The "few people about read the [warning notices on the bulletin] board and inquired for more particulars." Only a few Charlestonians attended Sunday morning worship services. Most heeded the warnings and stayed inside unless compelled to be out. Cirrus clouds were scudding across the sky, and the barometer was falling. Then, tiles went flying, and umbrellas were turned inside out and almost swept away. By 2 P.M. the slanting rain was so powerful it invaded the crevices of doors and windows.

Before sunset, the storm put the city into perfect darkness.[19]

---

[19] "The Storm! The Entire Southeast Suffers," *Augusta (GA) Chronicle*, August 29, 1893, 1.

On the water Sunday afternoon. A few Charleston families failed to prepare for the hurricane, but instead boarded their yachts on Saturday afternoon and sailed straight into it. They must not have seen the storm flags or read the bulletins. Like the group on Tybee Island east of Savannah, the yachting families were on a pleasure "excursion." One of the group was a family of five—mother, father, seventeen-year-old son, and two daughters, ages eleven and fourteen. Afterward, the mother, E. Rhett Lewis, recorded her unforgettable experience.

Anchored that Saturday night in the Stono Inlet behind Kiawah Island, they began to sense trouble. "The sun set in a lurid haze, and the wind was rising very steadily." Fitfully taking advantage of the rising tide early the next morning, two of the smaller yachts, facing the wind, headed back to port.

"[Sunday] morning broke, and the sun had abandoned us. A dull gray sky, clouds innumerable scudding wildly one after the other overhead, the wind now very high, and the tide coming in swiftly. At 7:30 our captain [husband/father] …determined to make use of the last two hours of the incoming tide and get as far up the river as it would take us….It was too late; the gallant *Winona* could no longer carry any sails at all. She careened over."

The wind rose higher and higher. At 1 P.M. the smallest yacht in the little fleet, *Collette*, managed to get up a small piece of canvas, Mrs. Lewis said, and tried to run before the wind into the Kiawah River to a place of safety.

> With anxious eyes we watched her staggering, lying down, dropping sail, raising it again, until she reached Kiawah and passed beyond our sight. The other yachts should all have followed her.

At two o'clock, the awful tide turned and began to rush in again, against the wind, and heaping up the maddened waters….

We dragged two anchors…until we were laying mid-stream, in the tremendous current, broadside on. Here the *Winona* rolled and pitched and wallowed…As each huge wave came rolling towards us,…Death looked us squarely in the face.[20]

Georgetown County. Edward Porter Alexander lived in South Island in Georgetown County, South Carolina, 120 miles up the coast from Savannah. The railroad president and former Confederate general took notes as he felt the approaching hurricane and as it ravaged his property. His "South Island log" entry for Saturday, August 26, said, "…worked all day at the barn. Wind easterly and fresh. At night became cloudy and fresher."

For Sunday, August 27:

Morning broke with wind from ne [northeast] and very stiff indeed. Boat went to get Episcopal minister for services tonight. At noon half a gale at least. Clear he not coming.

Worst coming. Two facts:

Barometer falling steadily, at morning, 29.60 inches, 6 P.M., 29.33 inches.

There would be a high tide at 8:06 P.M.

Miller house no longer safe. Water under it. Blow increased in intensity and rain was very heavy. ne [northeast] corner of house began to leak.[21]

---

[20]E. Rhett Lewis, "Yachting Experiences in a Cyclone," (Charleston SC) 1893, a personal account from family papers of William and John Bowen, 5.

[21]Edward Porter Alexander, South Island Log, 1835–1910, Manuscript Collection, University of North Carolina.

CHAPTER 3

"Dirty Weather" Turned Nasty

*The night has been unruly; where we lay our chimneys were
blown down, and, as they say, Lamentings heard in the air,
strange screams of death, and prophesying with accents terrible
of dire combustion and confused events.*

WILLIAM SHAKESPEARE

When the thrashing high tide continued to rise, charging into
the continent Sunday night, coastal dwellers began to realize
the horror of their predicament.

One group of vacationers, trapped on Tybee Island Sunday
afternoon, watched sand flying and water rising around their two
beach houses for a few hours before deciding they had better try to
get to safer lodging. They had a house of refuge in mind, but they
found it locked when they arrived. Next they went to the police bar-
racks, which they had believed to be a "strong building." It had
crashed in on itself. Their final refuge was another house, more than
a mile away.

"The water had risen so that the [railroad] track was covered knee deep and over," one of the group wrote later. "This time it was plunge in, or get out altogether, so in we went up to our knees. The wind was with us and just took us, or we would never have reached the house. The wind, sand, and rain were blinding us. People were fleeing to the woods to get into trees for safety as we passed along. Glancing back, we saw a house on fire, but we trudged on, little caring if it was ours or not."

The group of fifteen refugees including children spent the night in one room in a large house, wet and bedraggled, huddled together. They hung tightly onto the lantern so that when the crash came it would not be blown out, and they would "not have the horror of fire with all the rest." Water eight feet deep splashed against the exterior walls. "Every gust seemed more terrific—the intensity and force with which they struck the house seemed as though it must fall."[22]

Although the frightened people made it through the night and found the morning "clear and bright," what they found around them left them in near shock. "What desolation met us on every side—articles of every description, remnants of chairs, mattresses, baskets, trunks, pieces of furniture...." Finding the fourteen-mile-long train track demolished, in some places standing on its side like a fence, seeing the train's engine stopped dead still, with no track before it and no track behind it, they had no idea how they would get back to their homes in Savannah.[23]

"Mad ruin of the winds." The Morning News of Savannah reported that terror of a different sort reigned in downtown Savannah

---

[22]M. S. Workman, personal correspondence, September 2, 1893, from 154 1/2 Taylor St., Savannah GA typewritten paper, Manuscript Collection, Savannah Public Library.
[23]Ibid.

Sunday evening. "About 9 o-clock...the elements raged with ferocity. It was at the early stage of this increased fury that the arc-light wires...one after another went down from their fastenings. Wherever they fell upon or across other lines, luminous coruscations and often resplendent flames busy upon the peculiar gloom which shrouded the air..."

At the newspaper's headquarters on Bay Street where people were trying to gather, write, and typeset the news and run the presses Sunday night, "work was conducted with greatest difficulty." Since mid-afternoon, water had been pouring into the composing room and penetrating to the lower floors of the newspaper building. Rain wet the rolls of newsprint and the machinery, and it kept coming. After the electric lights went out at ten o'clock, the workers reactivated the old gaslights. When the motors that ran the presses quit working, they turned to their old boilers and engines.

For a time, as the hurricane's calm eye passed through the city, Savannahians could go outside, look up and see the stars. But the storm was not through doing its damage. The fury returned, as violent as before.

From Monday's headlines, it is clear that the reporters and editors felt a sharp sense of what they did not know for certain: "MAD RUIN OF THE WINDS. Savannah Swept by Terrible Hurricane. Many lives believed to have been lost. The Damage Beyond Estimate. Hundreds of buildings unroofed. One man instantly killed. Hutchinson's Island inundated. Vessels Wrecked at Tybee. Anxiety on the Railroads. Night of Terror in the City."

The next day's news report listed twelve other adults and three children killed during the night. Many had drowned. A falling roof had crushed one child. A six-year-old had been thrown from a floating housetop. One man had walked into a live wire on the street.

Along with the great lake of ocean water the hurricane threw onto the low land, the driving rain contributed mightily to the drenching and flooding everywhere. More than ten inches of rain turned Savannah's streets into streams and its roofs into sieves.[24]

"Not a green leaf." Still, the hurricane rammed its most powerful forces hard into the coast of South Carolina. The people of the Lowcountry heard its roaring cacophony and felt its raw destruction in various ways. At Beaufort County's Bluff Place on the Okatie River, about twenty miles from the ocean, one house lost two chimneys, its windows and its porch before the terrified Fripp family inside scrambled out and clung to the oak trees most of the night, surrounded by water waist deep.

Next morning, it was clear that the river itself had washed away so much of the bluff that the house looked like a dock. There was not a green leaf to be seen, the hurricane having stripped the trees as well as cracking off their limbs and uprooting many of the tree trunks. Many other houses on the property, a church, and all the outhouses had been demolished or swept away altogether. One had been saved by the trees that fell all around it and thus protected it against the wind.[25]

Elise Fripp filled her diary. "Would hardly know the place," she wrote. "The salt water is in the well, can't get any water, have to drink out of the ditch. We saved all of our cattle except eight goats. We have almost one hundred of Mr. Rice's sheep strewed along the bluff and seven dead cows. It is a sickening sight."[26]

---

[24] "Mad Ruin of the Winds Savannah Swept by Terrible Hurricane," *Morning News* (Savannah GA), August 28, 1893.1.

[25] Elise Fripp diary, Fripp Family papers, South Caroliniana Library, University of South Carolina, Columbia, SC.

[26] Ibid.

No Sunday night barometer or wind velocity readings are available from the town hardest hit by the hurricane. Beaufort sat on the high bluff overlooking the Beaufort River, about twenty miles north of Savannah, ten miles inland from the ocean. The Beaufortonians witnessed a normal high tide, then the storm surge and wind-driven breakers in the bay in front of the town. Beaufort's senator W. J. Verdier never forgot what he saw that night:

> The tide should have been high at 10:30 P.M. At midnight we still found it stationary. Then it suddenly rose two and one half feet higher and came in upon us with a sudden rush....
>
> The tide then rose fully eight feet above ordinary spring tide. The waves were twenty feet high in the town of Beaufort. The storm did not begin to abate until 3 A.M., when the tide began to ebb and the wind went to the south. When it did so, it wrought terrible destruction to the Bay area.[27]

Beaufort educator Rachel Mather wrote, "The wind rose higher and shrieked hoarsely, driven on with relentless fury, 'by the Prince of the power of the Air', till it sustained the fearful velocity of one hundred and twenty miles an hour and thus the hurricane raged without a lull for nearly fourteen hours. Nothing movable could stand before its sweeping power."[28]

C. E. Fripp of Beaufort in a Friday, September 1 letter to her sister wrote that the Parris Island quarantine station pharmacist, Jack Gowan Hazle, drowned Sunday night while trying to save the lives of two young black boys. "Oh, how sad, and what a loss to his

---

[27]"600 Lost on the Islands Frightful Fatality along the South Carolina Coast," *Morning News,* September 1, 1893, 1.

[28]R. C. Mather, *The Storm Swept Coast of South Carolina,* 3, Beaufort South Carolina County Library.

family. I hope he was saved," she added. "He never made a profession of religion." Then she added a note of worry about her family and friends: "Hope we will soon be relieved from the fear of want of food."[29]

Gone in a single night. Neils Christensen, a Denmark native who came to South Carolina after the Civil War, watched the ravaging of his Beaufort home and examined his damaged business properties the next morning. To his wife and son, who were in the Boston area at the time, he wrote a sorrowful letter from his place of refuge after the hurricane, Beaufort's Sea Island Hotel, battered but still standing.

> The storm started from the north and veered off to the northeast, then east. While in that direction, the upper part of the eastside piazza blew off, and half of that in front; then the tin roof was ripped off and carried into neighbor Seawall's lawn. Then the east chimney fell down and broke through the bathroom, the bricks falling on the floor and leaving a wide opening in the roof.
>
> The water rose over the wall and ascended the slopes to the house, when it spread and flooded the lawn…. The spray from the waves beat upon the piazza. Nearly every tree upon the grounds is blown down, and what are not destroyed that way will be by the salt water. Orange, fig, apple, peach, pear, plum, oak, willow, crape-myrtle, magnolia, and all the rest; the work of my hands these many years, gone in a single night…
>
> The cow was killed in the stable. The brick seawall I built years ago was leveled, and the soil, all the distance to the house, was licked and scooped away by the waves.

[29]C. E. Fripp, personal correspondence, September 1, 1893, Fripp Family papers, South Caroliniana Library, University of South Carolina, Columbia, SC.

In my lumber yard the same state of things exists. My lumber is scattered everywhere. The boilerhouse was destroyed, the boiler carried off by the waves and dumped some distance away. One of the $200 mares I bought some time ago lies in the yard drowned.

In my store there was eighteen inches of salt water standing on the floor this morning [Monday].[30]

Mr. Christensen's house was on the north side of town at the end of East Street, his lumberyard was on the Beaufort River at the end of Port Republic Street, his store at the corner of Bay and Carteret Streets.

C. Mabel Burn of Beaufort recalled the eerie feeling of watching the tide rise and rise and rise.

As night settled down, the wind increased in velocity and the tide was held up and could not fall, so the next tide piled on top of the first, and by midnight the ocean had come in over St. Helena and Lady's Islands and flooded Beaufort. The wind grew higher and higher, until it reached 125 miles per hour.

A second "tide" [the storm surge] having come in on top of the normal high tide and the wind walloping everything at 120 mph, the waves of the sea dashed against houses.... All small houses were washed away. Not one was left standing when the morning came.

Around 1 A.M. there was a furious ringing of our door bell, and a tall Negro man we know asked if he might bring women and children to our front porch as their houses were gone, and they had them in boats seeking shelter. My father said, "No. The

[30]Neils Christensen, diary, 1893, Christensen Family Papers, South Caroliniana Library, Columbia SC.

piazza is about to go as it is only held up by one column. Bring them into the house."

So in a room used as a private school room and equipped with benches and chairs, they were sheltered the rest of the night. Three trips of the big ferryboat [to Lady's Island] were made, bringing 12 to 15 people each trip so we had around 30 people sheltered for the night. They had lost everything they possessed except what was on their backs. When morning came, two old colored people, man and wife, were drowned, one lying at our front door, the other at the back.

Entire roofs of houses went whirling through the air to crash way back in town. All night this kept up.

Way in the worst of the storm we heard a crash, boards from a house on the next corner from ours, probably two hundred feet away, had been torn off and driven end ways through the side of our house. The house was so badly ruined we had to leave it when the storm was over.

Toward 5 A.M. the wind began to abate, and when daylight came, it was over. But what a wreck.[31]

Timber in the streets. Editor S. H. Rodgers of Beaufort's weekly, *The Palmetto Post* had no press on which to publish his newspaper immediately after the catastrophe. Undoubtedly overwhelmed with news to report and emotions to express, he penned hurricane stories for other publications.

… It would be impossible unless one published a volume, to tell half of what occurred.…

---

[31]C. Mabel Burn, "A Certified Correct Experience of Both Storms," quoted in Beaufort County Historical Society Paper #50, The Storm of 1893, attributed to Mr. And Mrs. W. O. Wall, no date, South Carolina Room, Beaufort Branch, Beaufort County Library system, Beaufort, South Carolina.

It was well known from telegraphic sources that a storm was about to break upon us, and everything in reason was done to protect against its fury, but scarcely one had an idea that it would last as long and destroy so much property as it has....

When darkness set in [Sunday night], the wind was blowing a stiff gale. As the hours of night sped on, the gale became more powerful, and trees began to shed their branches and foliage and fences commenced to fall before the blast.

At midnight the terror of the scene was added to by the rise of the tide to a height unprecedented....

Houses in all directions were swamped by the salt sea water, and the occupants were drenched from above from the rain which fell through the damaged roofs.

People were to be seen flying from tottering houses, and with trees falling and great timbers floating in the streets, and boards and shingles and tin flying in every direction, the scene was one never to be forgotten.

Then the wind changed to the southeast and from 2 A.M. till daylight the storm kept up, carrying the destruction in every blast.[32]

On Edisto Island between Beaufort and Charleston, inland behind two oceanfront barrier islands, old-time islanders realized that the weather outlook was ominous. Herbert Lee Bailey, a Charlestonian on Edisto that weekend on business, later told what he knew about the events there. "The day wore on, the wind rising higher, and higher, every moment, and towards afternoon the trees began to bend and sway in a terrible manner, branches and limbs flying in all directions," Mr. Bailey wrote. "By sunset we were all

---

[32]S. H. Rodgers, editor of (Beaufort SC) *Palmetto Post*, typewritten copy of story provided to other publications, 1893, 1, no date, South Carolina Room, Beaufort Branch, Beaufort County Library system, Beaufort, South Carolina.

thoroughly alarmed, and moved over to the 'Brick House,' deeming that the safest place to pass the night, and in an hour's time, the whole population of the village was gathered under its protecting roof, feeling thankful a safe shelter had been provided for us." "Brick House" had been built in the era of the American Revolution out of bricks imported from Holland, reputed to be extremely strong.

The Edisto Islanders' storm shelter withstood the hurricane's pounding. The next morning, however, brought a grim picture.

> What had been a smiling pretty village was nothing but a pile of wreckage and a mass of ruins.... As far as the eye could reach there was nothing to see but water and those spots from which the tide had receded covered with portions of houses, trunks of clothing broken open, and scattered, drowned poultry, & every crop ruined and prostrated.
>
> After a while we found some grist [grits] that had been saved by a colored man and cooking this with some salt water and drowned chicken, we subsisted till evening when help came in the shape of food and water.[33]

About thirty miles north of Edisto and seventy-five miles north of Savannah, the storm "put the city of Charleston in perfect darkness long before sunset," and waves flooded every street "below Tradd and Broad," said William A. Courtenay. He described Charleston's "visitor" as "ugly, unwelcome, and dangerous."[34]

---

[33]Herbert Lee Bailey, Red Cross field report 1893–94, Clara Barton Papers, Manuscript Division, Library of Congress, Washington, DC.

[34]"The Story of the Storm Sunday's Cyclone and its Ravages around the City," *News and Courier* (Charleston SC), August 29, 1893, 1.

An hour before midnight in Charleston, Mr. Jesunofsky left his
Weather Bureau office to see what was going on. He found the tide
covering all the wharves, and the water six to eight feet high over the
East Battery, where thick spray was "beating over the housetops." At
1:50 A.M. Monday, he ventured out again into the night and recorded what he called a "storm tide" (quiet water surface) at an East
Battery residence of 12.97 feet above Charleston Harbor's mean low
tide. His benchmark was the first riser on the steps on the Custom
House, downtown, where the water was 11.875 feet above mean
low tide, or about 2 feet deep in the street, indicating a storm surge
there of 6 to 9 feet.[35]

Meanwhile, in the mouth of the Stono Inlet south of
Charleston, E. Rhett Lewis' husband had cut the ropes to the
anchors being dragged by their sailing yacht *Winona* on Sunday
afternoon. Now, as the tidal waters inundated the marshes and
islands and the wind howled, the yachts bounced and pitched, out
of control.

"With the mad bellowings of the gale, the roar of many waters,
the fierce rush of the rain, not able to hear each other speak without shouting, we sped on in the fast-coming darkness, looking
eagerly for something—anything—to which we might cling," she
wrote afterward. At last the bone-weary and terrified boaters
plunged into a cedar tree, cracking a hole in the boat above the
water line. The father and son swung large ropes around the cedar
and lashed them to the foot of the mast.

"The darkness of the night was absolute, intense," Mrs. Lewis
recalled. "I plied them with small doses of whiskey, ginger, raw egg
rubbed up with sugar." At 3 A.M., the wind shifted, "thank God,"

---

[35] *Year Book, City of Charleston, 1893*, 249–51.

and seemed to come with less terrific force, the water began to fall, and the struggle ceased. They all dropped down just as they were and fell fast asleep.

Waking just as the sun rose, they found themselves aground on top of a small hummock, their craft tied to the only tree on it and surrounded by an "ocean of green marsh." Scanning the horizon, they discovered to their surprise that the whole bedraggled fleet had ridden out the monstrous storm, and, miraculously, not one life had been lost.[36]

Near Georgetown, Gen. Edward Porter Alexander recorded the barometric readings as they dropped steadily that afternoon until they began to rise again at 6:30 A.M. Monday. "Center of storm a little west of us," Alexander wrote early that morning. "Miller house props turned under and it came square down on the ground. Wind did not perceptibly abate until daylight. I slept 4:30 A.M. until 6 A.M. The tide was in the garden."[37] From the town of Georgetown itself, residents saw the Sampit River become a raging sea, its swollen tide having spread over dock and wharf, covering a large area of Front, Queen and Cannon streets to a depth of two feet.[38]

[36]E. Rhett Lewis, "Yachting Experiences in a Cyclone," (Charleston SC) 1893, family papers of William and John Bowen, 8.

[37]Edward Porter Alexander, South Island Log, 1835–1910 (Georgetown County, SC).

[38]"The Sampit River Described as a Raging Sea," *Morning News*, September 1, 1893, 5.

CHAPTER 4

The Ocean Rolled Ashore

"Death goes dogging everywhere."
W. E. HENLEY

For legitimate reasons, in the nineteenth century the islands along the Atlantic and Gulf coastlines of the Southeast were not considered desirable places to live. They were thought to be unhealthful. Mosquitoes and sand gnats swarmed on them. Summer days were hot and humid. The islands were exposed even more so than the rest of the coastal region to occasional high winds and flooding. And yet, until the night of the Great Sea Island Storm, Americans did not recognize the coastal islands as the dangerous places they could become in a hurricane.

At daylight Monday, August 28, the coastal folk from Savannah to Georgetown who had lived through the hurricane said gratefully to one another, "We are still here," and began to wander incredulously through the rubble.

Those who spent the night on the highest ground in the Lowcountry—away from the storm-surge zones—found a mess but few fatalities on the morning after. They did not know whether the inhabitants of the low islands between them and the Atlantic Ocean had ridden out the storm in safety or succumbed to it. Even a week later, a *New York Herald* reporter wrote that with "all the boats and flats gone, except when an occasional foot traveler comes into town, there is no getting any authentic description of what has happened in the remote places." Among the Charleston merchants and brokers, anxiety erupted over the condition of the island farmers' long-staple cotton and the river plantations' rice. If the crops were ruined, how would these businessmen collect the debts owed them? "On every tongue," said William A. Courtenay of Charleston, "is the question: 'What have you heard from the islands?'"[39]

By the time local and state officials were able to find out what the hurricane had done to the residents of the islands, the Gullahs were too hungry and too pitiful to do anything but pour out their night-of-the-storm stories.

No wonder men's hearts failed them with fear as they heard the thundering and roaring. No wonder they were paralyzed with terror as they saw trees, fences and their own chimneys falling before their eyes; no wonder, they were struck with consternation as they beheld the huge monarchs of the forest twisted like ropes and writhing in agony as they fell prostrate; and when they witnessed the tumultuous sea tearing away the shores and overwhelming the islands, is it strange they became too confused and dazed to make any wise effort for shelter and safety, or that

---

[39] "It Is Terrible Sea Islands Strewn with Dead Bodies," *New York Herald*, September 3, 1893, 1.

they believed the world had come to an end and this was the general breaking up and destruction of all things?"[40]

The islands' survivors told of tying their children to tree tops to keep them from drowning, of cabin homes that simply disappeared that night, of their boats that had been washed ashore and broken up in the pounding waves. They wailed over their revulsion and grief, having had to bury the rotting bodies of their family members, neighbors and livestock in the waterlogged soil. They explained in Gullah how the salt water that covered so much of their land had soaked the cotton in the fields and the corn in the cribs and had spoiled the sweet potatoes in the ground.

St. Helena: "Made a ruin." On St. Helena Island, the Penn School became a repository of unforgettable stories of personal hurricane experiences. Many of the island's residents did not make it through the night. From the archives of the Penn Community Services Center, as the Penn School campus is now called, comes a narrative from a seventeen-year-old Gullah boy whose brother, "Bubba," was four years old.

> De win' blow so hard dat day, an' when the night come, you ain't man fit stan' up' gin um. Now de rain come, an' I nubber see sich rain like dat since I bo'n. Ma and Pa and we all chillun been in de house. Pretty soon he begin for rock, and den de door bus' open, and we can't shut um.
>
> De moon been big, but blown up wid cloud, but you kin see little bit, and when I look out de tide up to de door, and seem like you kin see de whole ocean. Den de water come in de house, and we huddle under stairs. Man! De house rock awlful. An' we so scare.

---

[40]Rachel Mather, *The Storm Swept Coast of South Carolina*, 8.

Den crash and down come de house on top we all. Den such a fight and struggle. I ketch onto Bubba and hole him tight and every time I try an' get free de house strike me hard, but I ain't give up.

Well, we fight, and de wind blow so hard, and the wave so high I mos' give up myself. Pa 'courage we, and tell Ma, "Don't give up."

Ma mos' beat out and Pa have a battle wid de house. He weak too. De nex' wave strike Ma and knock him [her] out Pa han', and 'fore he could catch um, her gone, and we ain't see her no more.

Jus' Pa, Bubba and me…and if daylight been little longer, I had to give up.

But I save Bubba, and now all is jus' Pa, Bubba and me. Pa, he most broken down all to geder [altogether] most….[41]

A Penn School's annual report tells of an island community, "prosperous and happy," thirty years after the end of the Civil War, "made a ruin" by the "terrible calamity" of one night in 1893:

A cyclone came raging up from the seas of the West Indies and drove the tide before it in white crested billows over the greater part of the low-lying coast islands….

And yet, that night of howling hurricane, proved them men, with courage to do and dare as well as in any battle field [sic]. There was no panic rush for life, no cowardly desertion of women and children.

---

[41]Untitled, undated document, Manuscript Collection, Penn Center, St. Helena Island SC. The original document, recorded by J. Ross McDonald of St. Helena Island, respectfully attempts to capture the sounds of the Gullah language. Readers puzzled by the Gullah dialect as recorded may find that reading it aloud makes it easier to comprehend.

One father put his family into a boat that was driven upon the waves and guiding it into a thicket, kept them safe till morning.

One man, feeling his house quiver and lift, took his ax and cutting a hole in the floor let the water in to weigh down his house. He saved thus twenty lives.

One man put ox chains out at one window, round a tree stump, in at another window, fastened them together, so saving his family and house.

A father buttoned his baby in his coat, that his hands might be free, to help his wife and two children. Twice waves went over him, and great was his relief when reaching safety, he found the little thing still alive.

Another, looking out of his door, saw the water surrounding him. He looked once at his two children, playing on the floor, lifted them into the bed; told them to be good children, say their prayers and go to sleep.

Then, wrapping his sick wife in a blanket, he carried her out, plunging waist high through the waves and hearing the crash as his house fell over.

Bitterly his poor wife cried when she found he had saved her instead of the children.

"It was a hard thing to choose," the poor man said…with tears in his eyes.[42]

Frightful fatalities. Viola Chaplin, a member of the Penn School class of 1898 who spent the night of the hurricane on St. Helena, wrote a paper titled "The Cyclone."

---

[42]*Penn School Annual Report of 1898* (St. Helena Island SC), 5.

I will never forget as long as I live, how our island was overflowed with water, and we had nowhere to look for help, but [to] our Lord....

Our island was almost submerged. It was 12 feet deep in some places. Houses were shaken and floated by in the water, and there was a violent commotion everywhere.

One man took his wife and children on his back, one by one, and put them up in a big oak tree and there they remained until morning.

I heard of another man who was taking his family in a large oak tree in the same way. He took his children first, thinking that his wife could protect herself better than the little ones, but when he hurried back for her, there lay his poor wife, knocked dead by the fallen limbs of the trees. Wasn't it sad?

But I cannot tell all the sad things that happened that night before the wind changed and the tide ebbed...

Next morning we found our kitchen and all our outbuildings [at Penn School] were gone, swept away by the tide. Only a few houses were left. So many trees were blown down that we found it very difficult to get about. For nearly a month, the men were constantly clearing up the logs that fell across the roads.

Our crops were all drowned out. A few people who lived on the highest land saved a little, even potatoes. But most of us lost all.

The next morning there was not a chimney left on the place and before noon everyone was looking for some dry place to cook a little of what the storm had left them. When the daylight came to us after that dreadful night, it seemed as if we were in a strange country. Nothing looked like our old St. Helena.[43]

---

[43]Viola Chaplin, "The Cyclone," handwritten paper, Manuscript Collection, Penn Center, 1–2.

For the rest of the world, even in the Lowcountry, not until the Friday after the Sunday night hurricane did the magnitude of the disaster on the islands begin to emerge. The Savannah newspaper carried the headline "600 LOST ON THE ISLANDS. Frightful Fatality Along the South Carolina Coast." The story under it was grim:

> …The beaches, the undergrowth, trees and shrubbery, the marshes and the inlets, are turning up new dead bodies every time an investigation is made…. Some of the people, and they are among the best of this section of the state, even place the loss at more than 1,000….
>
> As the waters recede and the people move deeper into the wreckage gathered by the storm, the ghastly pictures are uncovered. So frequent are the discoveries that the finding of a single body attracts no attention at all. It takes the discovery of at least a group of half dozen or more to induce the people to show any feeling whatever.
>
> This section of the Atlantic coast has been prolific in storms—storms that scattered death and the destruction of property in their wake—but the weatherwise, the oldest citizen, the [river] pilot cannot recall anything equaling it….
>
> The seas ran high, and salt water waves were driven by the heavy winds as much as twenty miles inland. Houses were blown away. Trees were torn from the earth, leaving holes big enough to hide a freight train in. Vessels were dashed against the breakers, and thrown upon the earth as much as five miles from the water's edge….
>
> The wind alone was a storm which would have terrorized any community, but with the blinding rain and vivid flashes of lightning and deafening peals of thunder, the hearts of the stoutest were made to quail….

At first [on the morning after], no one thought of giving attention to anything or anybody outside of his own needs, but as the dead bodies multiplied the Good Samaritan feeling grew, and by noon every one on the chain of islands had become a grave digger.

…The coroner was compelled to swear in…deputies. One of these deputies held an inquest over seventy-eight people, and while the inquest was being held, seventy-eight graves were being dug and seventy-eight dead bodies, swollen and fast decomposing, were awaiting interment at the hands of their white and colored friends who escaped death so narrowly….

Some of [the islands] have not been heard from at all, while on those which have "spoken," there has not been a single one which did not increase the dead roll.

On some of these the death rate was large, but in many instances the names of the dead cannot be ascertained, many of them being beyond recognition when found, while others were unknown because no one was present who could identify them…. Many of the bodies are picked up on an island where they did not live and therefore are unknown.[44]

Bodies in the marshes. By Saturday, the number of dead was estimated in the Savannah newspaper at more than 1,000, but neither reporters nor official deputy coroners had any way to find and count all the corpses. They were in the marshes, in tree limbs, under the piles of wood that has been cabins and barns and boats.

The entire chain of islands along the South Carolina coast from Tybee north is a scene of indescribable ruin. The only traces that many of the islands bear of ever having been inhabited are

[44]"600 Lost on the Islands Frightful Fatality Along the South Carolina Coast," *Morning News* (Savannah GA), September 1, 1893, 1.

the half buried ruins of houses, the decaying bodies that lie in the sand and mud and are washed up by every tide, the thousands of dead cattle and the remnants of ruined crops.

The dead are buried as fast as they are found, without coffins or even a box. Hundreds of bodies lie in the mud, where they are washed up by the tide, and the earth is thrown over them or they are rolled into trenches. It is impossible to dig graves. The stench from the bodies of the dead and of the decaying cattle and hogs and the rank vegetation rotting under the sun is almost unendurable....

The estimates of the lost are almost as varying as the wind.... Those who have been over a part of the devastated section say that 1,500 is not too high an estimate...

Only the most meager information is obtainable [even a week later]. The only means of getting from place to place is by rafts, and here and there a boat...[45]

Injury, illness, and loss. Reporter Joel Chandler Harris, who wrote the Uncle Remus stories, came to the islands to write about the "cyclone" for the February and March 1894 editions of *Scribner's Magazine.* The advantage of time and of access to varied sources of information led him to conclude that as many as 2,500 had lost their lives on the night of the storm and that another 500 died in the aftermath. The lack of drinking water, the shortage of food and the prevalence of mosquito-borne diseases and infections no doubt took a toll. In the first few weeks after the storm, the medical records showed 3,709 sick people, 2,542 of them with malaria.

Harris offered *Scribner's* readers a plausible, picturesque reason for the long gap between the night of the disaster and the reporting

[45] "The Dead Beyond Number Buried in Trenches by Fifties," *Morning News*, September 2, 1893, n.p.

of it so that victims could be helped: "No other portion of the continent is so secure in its isolation."

The storm victims' predicament "must be described," he wrote, "and to be described it must be approached as the Sea Islands themselves are approached, by sinuous channels that turn upon themselves and wind in and out and lead in unexpected directions. The facts of the situation do not lie upon the surface....All the reports of the great storm are of a fragmentary character.... The impression left seems to be as vague and as shapeless as the tempest was."

Harris asked one island woman whether any of her children had been drowned in the storm.

> "How dee gwan drown, suh?" she answered, laughing. "I up'd de tree," she said, after a pause, with a gesture that explained how she saved them. "Dee choke—dee strankle—I up'd de tree!"
>
> Then the woman turned and pointed to another woman who was standing apart by the water's edge, looking out over the lonely marshes. "She los' dem chillum, suh. She have trouble."
>
> And so it turned out. This woman, standing apart, as lonely as the never-ending marshes, had lost three children.
>
> She had five.
>
> In the fury and confusion of the storm, she had managed to get them all in a tree. The foundations of this place of refuge were sapped, and the tree gave way before the gale, plunging the woman and her children into the whirling flood. Three were swept from under her hands out into the marsh, into the estuary, and so into the sea. They were never seen any more.
>
> She had nothing to add to this story as brief as it is tragic. One moment she had five children clinging to her; in another moment there were only two.

This woman, however, was "glad to God" to have two children left. She told Harris the story of a neighboring family. She showed where the house had stood, but there was nothing to mark its site, save a blackened stone that had lain in the fireplace. Thirteen had lived in that cabin. The entire family had been swept away.

As Harris observed, to get the picture of the size and power of the hurricane as it laid waste the islands, one must piece together the fragments of information that blew around afterward like so many random rooftops, plow handles, and tattered garments.[46]

Drifting and collapsing houses. Captain L. A. Beardslee was in charge of the Port Royal naval station, on what is now the Parris Island Marine Recruit Depot in Beaufort County, when the storm hit. The residents at the time, most of them black, totaled about 500. By the time Captain Beardslee and his wife traveled north in the fall, he had his personal story, as well as a part of the region's story to share with Northerners who wanted to know what had happened.

Houses came down like card houses. Some collapsed and crushed their inmates on the spot; others went drifting off with men, women, and children clinging to them, until falling to pieces, they dropped their living freight into eternity.

Some escaped by seeking shelter amid the branches of the giant pines and oaks; some were so saved, but others had but found death traps, for yielding to the force of the wind, many were thrashed to death by the whipping branches, or knocked off into the raging sea below.

I knew nothing of what was occurring on other islands than the one we were dwelling on, Parris Island, where I am in com-

[46]Joel Chandler Harris, "The Sea Island Hurricanes," *Scribner's Magazine*, 15 (February 1894): 241–42.

mand of the naval station; for, deprived of every means of communication with the outer world by the destruction of all railroads and steamers that connected with us, all of my boats either sunk or wrecked, our own affairs had my entire time and attention.

My house is a two-story frame, built on brick piers, about sixty rods [330 yards] from the beach. Between it and the water were six Negro cabins and two quite large houses. Shortly after sunset the weaker of them succumbed. My men succeeded in saving from the wrecks the women and children, all of whom were carried first to the largest of the two houses.

At about 11 P.M. the tide was at its height, and there came driving onto my lawn and under my house great timbers, wrecks of houses, wharves, and boats, and fortunately a large flat boat called a lighter. Some of the braver of my men captured this boat, by plunging in up to their necks, and pushed and pulled it to the house where the refugees had gathered, at which time the screams told us there was trouble. They got there just in time to rescue about fifty and brought them to my house.

The rescued islanders spent the night terrified, cold, and wet. By morning thirst and hunger would take over. Captain Beardslee's men bailed and pumped the cistern, then fashioned gutters and pipes out of weatherboards from a shed and servants' quarters—to capture the rainwater for drinking. But the food supplies in the Beardslee household and the home of the naval station's civil engineer, despite having been refurbished on Saturday before the Sunday storm, were a meager stock for the hundreds of people who would need to be fed. Even as the hurricane raged, the captain of the Parris Island naval station could see a food famine coming.[47]

---

[47] "In the Hurricane The Terrible Storm That Swept Over [the] Sea Island[s]," *Evening Star* (Washington DC), December 14, 1893, story credited to *Journal and Courier* (Little Falls NY), November 28, 1893.

CHAPTER 5

What Little They Had Was Wrecked

The storm has gone over me; and I lie like one of those old oaks
which the late hurricane has scattered about me. I am stripped of all
my honours; I am torn up by the roots, and lie prostrate on the earth!
EDMUND BURKE

ollar estimates of damage, no matter how precisely they
might be calculated, could not tell the whole truth of the
Great Sea Island Storm. What do abstract figures mean to a man
who lost his ox in the hurricane and has no beast to plow his field?
For islanders whose land would have sold for less than one dollar an
acre—if it could be sold at all—how does one assess the loss of a
mammoth chunk of sodden soil that tumbled over a bluff into a
tidal creek? In a region once lush with natural forests, how does one
tally the reduction in assets after hundreds of thousands of trees
have been broken off half way up the trunk or wrenched from the
ground? When all the cabin homes on an island are swept away in
a single night, with nothing left but blackened hearths to mark the

spots where they had once stood, who would dare guess at the total value of the damage?

The survivors had been terrified while the storm raged. They must have wailed at daylight as they looked over the consequences of it. Many did not know where their next meal would come from or where they would spend the night.

Rachel Mather's words about the Beaufort area could have been written about the whole region: "When the morning dawned… the fruitful fields all ready for harvest had become a desert waste. Immense heaps of seaweed and sedge were piled up far inland, and the shores were thickly strewn with wrecked vessels and household goods as far as the eye could reach. Fruit and forest trees were lying prostrate. Death and destruction seemed triumphant all around."

It would be impossible for anyone to have itemized all the losses even in a single small settlement of the Lowcountry. The hurricane had haphazardly dismantled some features of the landscape and obliterated others. Nothing in its path had escaped the hurricane's impacts altogether. What follows are examples of the damage.

Georgia. Coastal Georgians south of Savannah reported no deaths but many downed trees, smashed boats, undermined sea walls, lifted roofs, and shattered glass everywhere.[48] Brunswick's largest pilot boat was turned bottom up, the watchman and family of seven having been rescued during the storm the night before. On Jekyll Island a large unknown schooner had washed ashore; on St. Simons a sea wall had been torn apart.

Savannah's eighteen-mile distance from the ocean and her location on a high bluff gave her some protection. Still, evidence of freaks of the storm lay everywhere, according to the *Morning News*

---

[48]Pleasant A. Stovall, "The Cyclone in the South," *Harper's Weekly* 32 (September 16, 1893): n.p.

of Savannah. "[Savannah's] parks and shade trees, the most beautiful in the South, were damaged; the naval stores' docks were inundated; roofs along the bay were torn away"; the Tybee Railroad, seventeen miles long, was almost a total wreck. A schooner had dragged with its anchor several hundred yards of railroad track into the woods. Steel rails had been wrapped like hairpins around giant oaks. A boat had been impaled upon a prop. The Tybee quarantine station, called one of the finest stations in the South before the storm, was reduced to "nothing" that night.[49]

"Roofs [in Savannah] hung from the walls of buildings or were piled in the streets and on the sidewalks…. The churches did not escape the storm"—the damaged structures included a turret on St. John's, a ceiling on St. Patrick's, glass windows at Sacred Heart, the First Presbyterian's tower," and more.

Savannahians felt great affection for the *City of Savannah,* a finely appointed steamship, 2,550 tons and 272 feet long. What had happened to the vessel, supposedly on its way to the city from Boston, they could only guess. She failed to arrive on Monday as scheduled.

Hutchinson Island, a site recently developed as a major trade and tourism center for the twenty-first century, presented "a scene of devastation" Monday morning. "The entire island [was] still covered with water," as were the other low lands adjacent the river, the Savannah newspaper said the next day. A dairy farmer had gone to Hutchinson to try to get his cows out of the marsh and onto high ground. Although reported to be an excellent swimmer, he had drowned, and his family members assumed that rain and spray must have suffocated him. Sunday night, and at mid-week, others who lived and worked on the swampy islands and peninsulas between

---

[49]Ibid., 882.

FIG 5. Steamship City of Savannah, wrecked off Fripp Island,
Source: Harpers Magazine 1894

FIG 6. Waves wash over the City of Savannah, Source: Schein Files

South Carolina's New River and the Savannah River were missing and presumed dead.[50] The Savannah newspaper estimated at least 100 dead by Thursday, but with all the bridges demolished and the roads blocked by debris, there was no way to know for sure.

Bluffton and Daufuskie. Five men from Bluffton in southern Beaufort County—George C. Heyward, J. C. LeHardy, J. A Huger, and a Mr. Stevens and a Mr. White, who sailed to Savannah on Tuesday—told a reporter there of the damage they had seen. Along the way, they had found three schooners run aground—Vineyard, Mary, and John. As the hurricane raged Sunday night, Bluffton's May River had risen nine feet above spring tides, washing away a part of the bluff, undermining trees, and shoving the steamer Alpha ashore, breaking her windows. The wind had wrenched off roofs and had denuded and uprooted trees. However, situated on a high bluff, the village of Bluffton about nine miles from the ocean had escaped the hurricane's worst wrath.[51]

It may have been the Bluffton men who told a reporter about the night of the storm on Daufuskie Island, across Calibogue Sound from Hilton Head Island. Some of what happened there is described in *The Morning News.* As the hurricane's eye crossed Savannah and Savannahians observed the stars and an eerie calm, the eyewall of highest winds apparently passed west of Bluffton and Daufuskie Island. One man who was on Daufuskie at the time reported the water was two feet deep around the houses on the western side of the island; and about twenty-five feet of the bluff broke off there. The "Melrose" property on the Calibogue Sound side of

[50]"Cyclone of Death," *Morning News* (Savannah GA), August 29, 1893, 1.

[51]"Anxiety for Bluffton, The Steamer Edith Gone to Look after the Alpha," *Morning News*, August 29, 1893, 4.

Daufuskie—at the time a cotton plantation—had lost 100 feet of bluff near the main house, including half of a beautiful garden.

The "Daufuskie Range" lighthouse on the northeast corner, presumably on Haig Point, was "dilapidated." "One of the most remarkable effects of the beating of the seas was shown at the high bluff on Daufuskie Island. This bluff [is] seventy-five feet high and about 700 feet long. The force of the waves…washed away the entire bluff for thirty feet back…" the newspaper reported Wednesday.

By Friday's edition, more bad news had come to light about Daufuskie. The keeper of the Bloody Point lighthouse told of his family's harrowing Monday morning escape from their home as the "seas dashed clean through the house." Wading in water waist deep, he had carried his children and led his wife three-quarters of a mile to another building. By the time the worst storm conditions had subsided, they realized the station was a near total wreck. The kitchen, oil room, and boathouse had been torn from their foundations and two buildings had washed 500 yards up on the island.[52]

All of Daufuskie's cultivated land was ruined. For the island's inhabitants, the loss was complete, and it was clear they would suffer from want of the necessities of life.

"The Negroes on [nearby] Pine Island [across Ramshorn Creek from Daufuskie], which has been deserted by white people since the storm of 1881, passed the night in their boats under the live oaks. The whole island was under water."[53]

Hilton Head Island. As for Hilton Head Island, the second largest island on the Atlantic coast with a population of about 2,500, news of what had happened there was scarce or non-existent

---

[52] "At the Bloody Point Lighthouse," *Morning News*, September 1, 1893, 8.

[53] "The Storm at Daufuskie The Inhabitants Spend the Night in Anxiety," *Morning News*, August 30, 1893, 3.

FIG 7. Ships on shore near Beaufort, Source: Schein Files

FIG 8. Digging out in Beaufort, Source: Schein Files

in the early reports. Finally, in mid-October almost two months after the hurricane, a *New York World* reporter interviewed Dr. John MacDonald, the American Red Cross agent stationed there.

On Dr. MacDonald's initial inspection of Hilton Head, he said, he found 304 families, 1,285 people, in need of assistance. He described appalling conditions:

> Those whose corn was entirely destroyed by the salt water were still eating it, having nothing else. This accounts for much of the stomach trouble I found. I advised them to burn what was rotten and issued grits to them to replace it.
>
> With the exception of two wells…there is no water on either Hilton Head or Pinckney Island fit to drink, all of it being brackish….
>
> There are a great many cases of malaria of more or less acuteness, and a majority of the people are suffering from what I term "storm sickness," i.e., contusions, colds, rheumatism, etc., the effect of exposure….
>
> These people are destitute of bedding and wearing apparel, their houses in many cases being entirely washed away.
>
> Many people are sleeping in the open air on the ground….We need lumber, nails, hatchets, and saws badly.[54]

The islands. On hard-hit St. Helena Island—where the population had been about 6,000 before the storm—the scene on the morning after was shocking:

> The people, prosperous and happy on Sunday morning, stood on Monday beside their dead, bewildered, homeless, with-

[54]John MacDonald, Red Cross field report, 1893–1894, typewritten copy, 2, Manuscript Collection, American Red Cross.

out food, without a change of clothing, with absolutely nothing....The cotton had disappeared, the corn and potatoes lay buried in the mud....

Stores and houses had been swept away like chaff. Great forest trees lay uprooted across the obliterated roads. Salt sedge, entangled with dead bodies, broken wreckage, drowned animals, was piled high almost to the centre of St. Helena....

Harder by far was it for the living than for the dead! [55]

No doubt similar scenes of desolation existed on the nearby islands. Datha (now called Dataw) and Warsaw each had about 100 residents before the storm.

On Lady's Island, where about 2,000 lived in 1893, corpses were laid into mass graves. "The bodies are evidently buried just below the surface and emit a deathly and sickening smell," a Charleston reporter wrote. "The dead were buried all last week, and boxes made out of the wrecked lumber took the place of coffins.... As many as six are in one grave."[56]

Fearing the outbreak of disease from the decaying flesh, health officials ordered more earth to be put on the graves and arranged for a supply of disinfectant to be sent to Lady's Island at once. For a while the survivors and deputy coroners tried to keep track of the names of the dead on all the islands, but they finally gave up. It was more important to get the bodies into the ground than to count them.

Nor could a Charleston reporter trying to gather information get a solid fatality count. He did come to understand the horror of the catastrophe, however, as he was rowed in a small boat from Beaufort to Lady's Island. "The trip across was pleasant enough," he

[55]*Penn School Annual Report, 1898*, (St. Helena Island SC), 5.

[56]"Seeing Is Believing A Tour of Inspection of the Sea Island [s]," *Post and Courier* (Charleston SC), September 6, 1893, 1.

FIG 9. Downtown Beaufort after the 1893 hurricane, Source: Schein Files

FIG 10. Craven Street in Beaufort after the hurricane, Source: Schein Files

FIG 11. Where F.W. Scheper's warehouse once stood in Beaufort, Source: Schein Files

wrote, "although we had to listen to the sorrowful tale of the boat-
man, Albert Brown, who on Sunday night was at home with his
wife and child and is today is the only survivor of that little
family."[57]

Beaufort and Port Royal. Monday found massive destruction on
Port Royal Island, which had 3,500 living in the city of Beaufort
and 3,000 residents in the rural areas and the smaller town of Port
Royal. Editor S. H. Rodgers of *The Palmetto Post* is believed to be
the author of a typewritten paper on the story: "All the docks were
entirely demolished, and the timbers strewn in every direction. The
large warehouse of F. W. Scheper [on the riverfront], with its contents, was broken to pieces, and the debris was taken up to and
beyond the courthouse." Scheper's family had escaped, and he was
philosophical about his loss:

> Mr. [William] Marscher had a narrow escape in getting his
> wife, Mr. Scheper's daughter, out of their home over the ware-
> house. The steps were blown away, and they had to wade in four
> feet of water during the height of the storm.
>
> "Well," Mr. Scheper said after surveying the destruction, "I
> made a mistake. I put the big warehouse in the wrong place. If I
> had known this storm was coming, I would not have done that.
> It took me about 15 years to make what I have lost, but I am bet-
> ter off in experience, and in ten years, I will make it again. I don't
> see anything to despair about."

Actually, Mr. Scheper had lost three warehouses and two wharves,
had sustained the wreckage of his two pilot boats and most of the

---

[57]Ibid.

fifteen houses he owned. As a victim of such damage, he had plenty of company.

"The cotton gins and gin house, and the warehouses of Waterhouse and Danner in Beaufort [also] were destroyed with their valuable contents of Sea Island cotton and heavy groceries…. The elegant office and complete law library and valuable papers of Hon. W. J. Verdier are a complete loss. Not a vestige remaining save the iron safe which stands in a pool of water…." On and on the distressed editor continued. Houses had been unroofed. A gristmill, stored grain and hay and rice, the drug store, and the jewelry store had been badly damaged. The flooded courthouse had lost its windows and its roof. Tugs had been blown aground, as well as the *Pilot Boy*, a steamer found a quarter of a mile inland. Every bathhouse had disappeared. St. Helena's Episcopal Church, recently refurbished, had its roof blown off and its interior soaked.

In the nearby town of Port Royal, "a scene of desolation," all fences and outhouses had disappeared, and every home was damaged. "The residence of J.K. Attaway was torn from its underpinnings by the force of the water and wind, and the debris striking against it, and was demolished. The lower story gave way, and the upper came hurtling down."

"When daylight came, what a wreck," wrote C. Mabel Burn. "The [Beaufort] waterfront was a shambles…. Every street in town was piled as high as the house tops with uprooted trees, demolished houses, household furniture, etc…. Almost all houses depended on cistern water for the homes, and these were filled with salt water…. For weeks fires were kept burning in the streets and the dead bodies of dogs, chickens, etc., were burned, for they could not be buried."

Ms. Burn wrote her account as a "certified…correct experience" of the 1893 storm. She remembered it in November 1959—after

FIG 12. Devastated Beaufort waterfront after the 1893 hurricane, Source: Schein Files

FIG 13. Atlantic Wharves in Charleston destroyed, Source: Harpers Magazine 1894

FIG 14. New Ashley River bridges in Charleston wrecked,
Source: Harpers Magazine 1894

Hurricane Gracie had battered Beaufort. She said at the time that Hurricane Gracie had done her best to demolish the town but had failed, largely because Gracie "did not have the help of the ocean that [the Great Sea Island Storm] did…."[58]

C. E. Fripp of Beaufort, who wrote the immediate news of the storm to her sister September 1, followed up with descriptions on the twenty-sixth. Many cisterns remained unusable, and many houses still had not been repaired a month after the hurricane. She knew of Beaufort residents suffering "from stomach complaints." She had heard of the discovery of a live five-foot shark in "the churchyard," although she did not say which churchyard. By then she had heard that in the courthouse floor and the jail, the water had risen to the height of a man's chin.

"When I think of the distress of some of my dear friends," she wrote, "my heart aches for them."[59]

Industry destroyed. Coosaw Island had a population of about 200 before the hurricane. Nearby Chisolm's Island had about 300 residents. No newspaper accounts tell the stories of those islands on the night of the storm or afterward; however, what happened to the phosphate fleet hints at the kinds of traumas those communities must have faced.

> On Monday morning after the storm, the scene beggared description. [Beaufort County's] Coosaw River and the Sea Islands appeared as if a conflagration had swept the earth and destroyed or withered everything. Looking down Coosaw River…, not a living object could be seen, not a craft afloat, but

---

[58]C. Mabel Burn, "A Certified Correct Experience of Both Storms," November 3, 1959, type-written copy, Manuscript Collection, Beaufort County Library.

[59]C. E. Fripp, personal correspondence, Fripp Family papers, South Caroliniana Library, Columbia SC.

here and there appeared a blackened crane or barnacle-covered bottom of a sunken dredge or wash boat. The mining fleet, the pride and support of the people of this part of the State, lay wrecked and ruined in the marshes and woods along the shores…for a distance of twelve miles….

None of the companies was insured except the Carolina Mining Company carried a policy…on *John Kennedy. John Kennedy,* a $300,000 dredge, was found a total loss on the morning after, the bodies of her "gallant" captain and crew found inside her hull.[60]

With no equipment, the phosphate mining companies discharged all their "hands."[61] For the thousands who had worked "on de rock," as the Gullahs referred to their mining jobs, and for the thousands of family members who depended on them, the hurricane had taken not only homes and loved ones, but work places and livelihoods also.

Coosaw Island had a population of about 200 before the hurricane. Nearby Chisolm's Island had about 300 residents. No newspaper accounts tell the stories of those islands on the night of the storm or afterward; however, what happened to the phosphate fleet hints at the kinds of traumas those communities must have faced.

In a terrain so intertwined with waterways, how does one appraise the value on a boat of any kind? There was no way of guessing in the region from Savannah to Charleston how many personal and commercial bateaux, barks, schooners, lighters, barges, and ships sank or were hurled ashore or beaten up in so many different ways they could never be recovered. The transportation system, so dependent on watercraft, had been bashed to bits.

---

[60]"The Sea Islands' Dead Inspector Jones Says Number Will Go Above 1,000," *Morning News,* September 3, 1893, 1.

[61]Ibid.

FIG 15. Debris in Council Street in Charleston,
Source: Harpers Magazine 1894

FIG 16. Thunderbolt near Savannah, Georgia, after the 1893 hurricane,
Source: Harpers Magazine

Steamship run aground. As the hurricane had traveled westward across the Atlantic, the 272-foot steamship *City of Savannah* had left Boston for Savannah on Thursday, August 24, with Captain George Savage in command. She had about thirty people aboard, including two children and the crew, and medium-size cargo. Starting out in a gale, the ship reached heavy seas from the southeast off Cape Hatteras Saturday, and by three o'clock Sunday afternoon just off the coast of Charleston was thrashing about in the teeth of the storm.

She lost her power, began to take water into the engine room and started drifting in the rough seas. By early Monday morning, she had been driven onto a sand shoal about 3 miles off Beaufort County's Fripp Island. As the passengers huddled together on the starboard side, she began to take on water, and the waves demolished the saloon and gutted the cabins. The passengers and the crew spent Monday night lashed in the rigging. "The waves dashed over them, and death was expected at every moment."[62]

On Tuesday morning, Captain Savage sent two lifeboats to St. Helena Island, carrying the *City of Savannah*'s women and children and two ship's officers to safe quarters there. Three riverboat pilots from Beaufort—John O'Brien, William VonHarten, and John L. Mack—tried to stage a rescue, using a tug with a 10-foot draft. Just as they realized the water was so shallow they could not reach the grounded ship, they saw the steamship *City of Birmingham* on the horizon and hoped she would be able to save the endangered crew and passengers.

At about six o'clock Tuesday night, the *City of Birmingham* anchored nearby. The water was too rough to attempt a rescue at that time, however, so the remaining passengers and crew spent another

---

[62] "Lost in the Breakers The City of Savannah Wrecked," *Morning News*, August 31, 1893, 1.

night lashed to the rigging with nothing to drink and only raw turnips to eat. At daybreak Wednesday, crews from the *Birmingham* began the rescue in earnest, and by noon, "those who had stared death in the face for thirty-six hours were safe aboard the *Birmingham*." Nearly crazed with thirst and dehydration, they asked first for water. Soon, they also had a meal—their first since mid-day Sunday. Captain Savage, the last man off the ship, carried a white cat with one blue eye and one brown eye with him as he walked ashore.

After the *Birmingham* delivered them to Savannah, the captain slept a few hours before going to St. Helena Island in a tugboat to get the rest of his passengers and two crewmembers. On Friday morning, when the tug delivered the captain, the women, and the children to Savannah, a crowd of 1,000 Savannahians applauded and cheered from the bluff overlooking the Savannah River.[63]

After the Great Sea Island Storm of 1893, the grandeur of the *City of Savannah* was no more. Attempts to salvage her failed. In a few years, she came to be called "The Wreck," a favorite fishing drop. Today sea bass and sheepshead feed on the barnacles that plaster her boilers, the only relics left of the once proud ship.

Charleston and Edingsville. A resort village between Edisto Island and the ocean, Edingsville Beach, virtually disappeared in the hurricane. Edingsville had been a summer community of about forty-two buildings, including two churches and a billiard saloon, on a narrow strip of sand. Twenty-four hours of pounding winds and waves destroyed most of what had been built there and most of the island itself. Successive storms later breached the remaining shoal and pushed the sands onto the marshes.[64]

---

[63] "Everyone Was Saved The City of Savannah's Survivors," *Morning News*, September 2, 1893, 1.

Early reports show fifteen deaths in Charleston, twelve from drowning and three from falling walls and roofs.[65] Having gone out into the night to see what the hurricane was doing to the city, Mr. Jesunofsky probably could have predicted what he would see the next morning. Nevertheless, looking over the debris at daylight, he must have been appalled.

"The scenes of wreckage which meet the eye are desolate in the extreme," he wrote.

> The once-beautiful promenade was totally undermined, although the solid seawall remains. All piers are stripped bare; the sheds are leveled. Three barks are total wrecks; many schooners and pleasure boats were beaten to pieces—literally ground up, so to speak—by the force of the wind and waves.
>
> The Market was flooded three to five feet. Some 10,000 or more bales of cotton, kept in storage… were damaged by the storm-tide. On the west side, yards were flooded to the depth of five feet; slate and tin roofs, shingles and cornices flew fast and thick…. The streets all over the city are piled high with debris….Freight cars were upset and blown far from the tracks."[66]

The city engineer reported that in addition to the wreckage of Charleston's buildings, docks, streets, and boats, "Eight hundred and ninety-six beautiful shade trees, belonging to the city, were blown down." He added, no doubt with regret, "This does not include the many hundreds which belonged to the citizens."

---

[64]Rhet Wilson, "The Beach That Was," *Coastal Heritage*, bulletin no. 6, n.d., (Charleston SC: SC Sea Grant Consortium) 6.

[65]"Blast of Death at Charleston," *Morning News*, August 30, 1893, 1.

[66]*Year Book, City of Charleston, 1893*, 249–50.

What else? "No birds were seen about Charleston until four days after the storm."[67]

At Grove Plantation off the Edisto River south of Charleston, 9 1/2 acres of rice that had been cut and were a total loss, all of the animals had been washed away except four mules and two horses. The plantation's overseer wrote to B. Grimball, the owner, that most of the water control devices in the rice fields had been "whipped off by the waves." There were many breaks in the "banks" (rice dikes). Spades, shovels, and wheelbarrows—the basic tools of rice-plantation construction and repair—were at the bottom of the river. "Please send by the first boat coming this way 12 wheelbarrows, 12 shovels, 12 spades, and corn for the animals. If no boat is coming, please send by railroad," he wrote. "Everything is in a fearful condition. Come as soon as you can."

"I am trying to get over the effects of the storm," L. M. Grimball Jr. of Pinebury wrote to his sister on September 21, three weeks after the hurricane: "I shall have to pull down the store and put up another. It will cost considerable money, what with the fence, the stable, and all so as to make me comfortable for a few more years." One of the saddest things was that Mr. Grimball had lost his dogs, Dan and Sheba.

As sorrowful as Mr. Grimball was and as concerned as he was for his own well-being, he also wrote of his worry about another member of his family. "He works so hard, always seems to meet calamity. The cyclone destroyed 3/4 of his buildings, and 250 acres of rice that had been harvested all went to Davy Jones."[68]

---

[67]Ibid., 253.

[68]L. M. Grimball, personal correspondence from Colleton County, Grimball Family papers Manuscript Collection, University of North Carolina Library.

A few days after the storm, fifteen Charleston rice planters scouting from the windows of a southbound train got "bluer and bluer" as they found "ruin, ruin on every side," according to their report. A sawmill twenty miles from the ocean had been demolished. Once "beautiful Beaufort" was filled with scenes "thoroughly demoralizing," they said.[69]

Rice, cotton, and corn on the stalks had been soaked by saltwater flooding or rain and wind-beaten to shreds.

South Carolinians helpless. Stripped of their rice and cotton to sell and their corn to grind into grits and meal and to feed to the livestock during the winter, the people of the South Carolina Lowcountry were helpless to help themselves. The destruction had put a pall on the region. But none of obvious wreckage compared in impact to the loss of lives and for those left the loss of food supplies. And yet, as stunned as they were by what had happened to them, even the most downcast coastal dwellers probably did not recognize the severity of the catastrophe. Help was not going to arrive soon, and even after it began to trickle into the region, normal living was more than a year away.

> The great questions that met our citizens on that first day were of appalling significance: How shall the famishing thousands be fed until relief comes? Where shall food be found and how transported hither? How shall the salt water be removed from the wells and springs so men and animals may quench their thirst? How shall all this debris with decaying animal and vegetable matter be removed—debris whose foul exhalations would quickly poison the air and breed an extensive pestilence?[70]

---

[69] "Out of the Depths: A Thrilling Story of the Storm's Awful Work," *Sunday News* (Charleston SC), September 3, 1893, 1.

[70] R. C. Mather, *The Storm Swept Coast of South Carolina*, 20, Historical Collection, Beaufort South Carolina County Library.

CHAPTER 6

Exposure and Starvation

Hunger allows no choice to the citizen or the police;
We must love one another or die.

W. H. AUDEN

T he first word from the Sea Islands reached South Carolina
Governor Tillman by telegraph from Yemassee Thursday night,
August 31—four nights after the hurricane raged through the
region. The railroad tracks were too damaged to handle trains, but
a railroad agent, J. H. Averill, had traveled twenty-four miles, walking from Port Royal to Whale Branch, crossing the river by boat,
and then continuing from there walking to the Yemassee train station to send the message.

The telegram described the Sea Islands as scenes of unprecedented desolation and pleaded for "speedy relief." The governor
declared the situation a severe emergency and urged immediately
that "all classes of people" make contributions of food, clothing,
money, and the other "necessaries of life."[71]

---

[71] "Gov. Tillman Appeals for Aid for Unfortunates of the Storm," *Morning News* (Savannah GA),
September 1, 1893, 1.

Robert Smalls, the state's first black congressman, by then out of office and serving as Beaufort's port collector, issued a general appeal at the same time, lamenting the many fatalities and the complete destruction of Beaufort's wharves and warehouses. He then added that the remaining residents of the Sea Islands, known for their thrift and industry, were in desperate straits, everything they owned having been swept away. "We earnestly ask for aid in feeding and clothing the hungry and naked," he said, signing his appeal, "Robt. Smalls, Collector and Chairman Citizens Committee."[72]

After the people of the state and the nation learned what the storm had done to the Lowcountry, they began to try to meet the needs—slowly, tentatively at first, unaware of the scope of the problems.[73]

The Morning News of Savannah reported Sunday, September 3, 1893, one week after the hurricane, that the islanders "are destitute of everything, even clothing, that rags barely cover their body. They do not need money; what they need is food and clothing to keep them alive." Neighbor began trying to help neighbor, but there was not enough of anything to go around.

Local relief committees formed in various neighborhoods. A "mass meeting of citizens" gathered in Charleston Saturday, six days after the hurricane, to "send relief to the sufferers on the Sea Islands.... Contributions were called for, and those present subscribed $1,500 at once."[74] (That would be the equivalent of about $30,000 in today's currency.) Beaufort's Sea Island Relief Committee, including Mayor George Holmes and Robert Smalls, organized itself into subcommittees. They began to try to gather

[72]Ibid.

[73]Ibid.

[74]"Planning Prompt Relief," *Morning News*, September 3, 1893, 1.

information and to provide necessities for the survivors, including those on the remote islands, large and small. They could not be sure of the needs immediately, but by the end of the week, they believed that about 800 lives had been lost and that 6,000 survivors needed food supplies right away.

The subcommittees established guidelines for the distribution of food, tents, medicines, and "supplies of whatever kind needed" and then appealed in writing to the American people. Rather than emphasizing the horror of the storm itself, they wrote simply, "There is not a grain of corn nor a pod of cotton left in the fields washed by the raging sea. The destruction was thorough and complete."[75]

One committee chairman wrote a general appeal: "A supply of Ruta Baga Turnip seed would be very serviceable at this time."[76]

A few spontaneous gestures staved off hunger pangs in the early stages of the aftermath. A representative of the Charleston-to-Savannah railway promptly offered to send provisions free of freight charges. Shortly, 2,500 loaves of bread, 25 pounds of corned beef, 100 boxes of soda crackers, 50 barrels of grits, and 5 barrels of molasses were on the way to Beaufort for distribution. Survivors from the outlying areas immediately began crowding into Beaufort, milling the streets, looking for food and assistance. Neither was coming fast enough to meet the growing demand.

Governor Tillman appointed Dr. J. W. Babcock, superintendent of the state lunatic asylum, as his emissary to the scene, saying,

[75]Appeal of the Sea Island Relief Committee, Manuscript Division, Library of Congress, Washington, DC.

[76]Governor B. R. Tillman, correspondence, September 14, 1893, Papers of Governor B. R. Tillman, South Carolina Department of Archives and History.

I want first an absolutely correct accounting of the losses on these islands and in this territory. I want to know exactly what houses are gone and what houses are standing. I want to know what has been done with the dead that have been there on the sands for a whole week.

I want to know if tents are needed to house the women and children who survived. I want to know if there is not danger of some epidemic breaking out and wiping out all the people there who have survived the war of the elements.

As curious and perhaps worried as the governor was, he also expressed a caution that prevailed widely even as the people of his state faced starvation: "We want to guard against those people who, seeing that aid is coming, might do nothing.... I do not want any abuse of charity."[77]

Let them eat fish. Although the governor expressed compassion and pleaded for donations from the public, he grossly underestimated what it would take to relieve the suffering and put the stricken people on the road to recovery. Racism certainly may have played a part in the attitude of the governor and others toward the storm's victims. A vast majority of them were black. Most spoke only Gullah. They lived on remote islands off the coast, not on mainland South Carolina.

The Democratic governor, mindful of his unpopularity in the Lowcountry in the last election, was generally unsympathetic to the citizens there—mostly Republicans. In addition, the governor had no background to enable him to evaluate the damage and alleviate the human suffering. He had no understanding of what a hurricane's storm surge can do to a community, no disaster relief training

---

[77]Ibid.

or experience and no culture that would have encouraged him to respond with the compassion, wisdom, and will so badly needed. He had no emergency relief department, no funds appropriated for the desperate needs the Lowcountry faced.

Nobody anywhere in the country had ever seen such devastation. Public resources had never been given to individuals for food, shelter, and clothing. Governor Tillman happened to be the chief executive of one of the poorest states in the Union during one of the worst national depressions in history.

"The people have the fish of the sea there to prevent them from starving," the governor said,[78] but they had no boats to go fishing—and probably no nets either, the storm having sucked everything they owned into its great maw and spewed it out half-digested. "Provided they can get a little bread from other sources, they can live where they are cheaper and better for the present than if we tried to transport them into some other section of the state…. They doubtless have their [sweet] potatoes left in the ground," he said.[79] Actually, the salt water had blackened the potato vines and rotted the crop.

"I hope, too, that someone will make them go to work at once and plant turnips on the islands. They can get them ready for winter, and it is the only crop that they can now raise. Provisions at Beaufort and other points there will run out, very likely, in a day or two," he said.[80] Yes, provisions were in short supply. And, yes, they could plant turnips if they had turnip seeds and if the water could be drained off their land. Even turnip seeds, though, require from forty to sixty days to produce food.

[78]Ibid.

[79]Ibid.

[80]Ibid.

The governor did urge private donors to come forward, with cash to buy food, "which could then be distributed by boats." He did not offer boats, however. Nor did he offer a plan for collecting funds and getting provisions to the desperate survivors.

South Carolina's Senator M. C. Butler appealed to the US Secretary of War. The Secretary pointed out that he had no power to issue rations to American citizens without an act of Congress authorizing him so to do. He said he would be glad to lend tents to the homeless.[81]

Despite the desperation of the people of the Lowcountry for food, shelter, and clothing, the governor was suggesting turnip seeds and the Secretary of war was offering only tents. If others had not come forward, starvation and illness would have done as much damage as the hurricane itself. Fortunately, J. J. Dale, a Beaufort area resident—for whom the Dale community was named—traveled north immediately after the hurricane to appeal for help. As a result, New Yorkers early on began to respond.

A week after the hurricane, Charleston's headlines began to tell of New Yorkers' generosity: "The North's Noble Heart…Relief Pouring In for the Sea Island Sufferers. Carolinians At Work Enlisting the Wealthy and Charitable of New York, Who Respond with Touching Promptness and Liberality."[82]

After six days of "vexation and suspense," the Western Union telegraph connection between Charleston and New York began to function again. Soon a steady stream of appeals for donations filled the telegraph wires. Newspapers from all of the country joined in, urging their readers to open their hearts and their bank accounts.

---

[81]Ibid.

[82]"Cyclones on Carolina Coast 1893: The Newspaper Accounts of The Great Storm of 1893 and Loss of Life," various newspaper clippings organized by William A. Courtenay, 1900.

From the *New York Tribune*: "He gives twice who gives quickly."

From the *New York Evening Post*: "The whole country ought to assume the attitude of brotherly protection promptly and gladly."

From the *Cincinnati Tribune*: "Cincinnati's commercial interests are too closely allied with the interests of the South to permit us to stand idly by."

From the *Jacksonville Times-Union*: "If ever a cause commended itself to the kindly impulse of the public, surely it is this. Hard times are no excuse for hard hearts."

The *New York World* not only appealed to its readers with words, it also commissioned a train that hauled boxes and barrels and crates of food and other supplies to the South Carolina Lowcountry.

Nonchalant state response. Three weeks after the hurricane, the governor and other state officials still failed to recognize that the Lowcountry residents and their one large industry, phosphate mining, were not going to spring back. Governor Tillman, with South Carolina's Board of Phosphate Commissioners, inspected the wreckage of the phosphate miners' equipment, found production stopped totally, and concluded that restoring operations would cost "a very large sum of money." Under his leadership, the phosphate board, however, offered nothing more than to reduce the per-ton fee to the state from one dollar to fifty cents between September 1893 and January 1894 for the mining companies that would "actively begin at once the work of restoration."

In 1894, the reduced per-ton fee also would apply, but only after the mining companies together had paid at least $75,000 to the state to meet bond obligations.[83] The reduction of state fees

---

[83]South Carolina General Assembly, Board of Phosphate Commission, *Third Annual Report to the General Assembly of the State of South Carolina at the Regular Session of 1893* (Columbia SC, 1893), 4.

under those conditions constituted "all the concessions possible" to the phosphate industry, the governor said.

In essence, the state told the phosphate miners to get back to work immediately and send $75,000 to the state. These were the miners whose dredges and barges were on the bottom of the Coosaw River, whose wharves and sheds were demolished, whose dredge crews and phosphate divers had nowhere to live and nothing to eat. At least one other appeal went from the scene of the disaster to the governor—and was turned down. Ellen Murray, co-founder of the Penn School on St. Helena Island and superintendent of the St. Helena Temperance Society, made her case in a letter from Milton, Massachusetts, September 17, 1893: "As a resident for thirty years on St. Helena, I am well acquainted with the needs and habits of the Negroes there. They have been an industrious, self-supporting people, caring for their sick and aged, raising on their small farms of ten to thirty acres the provisions for their families and putting the rest of their 'force' into cotton...."

After assuring the governor that the St. Helena community heartily supported the temperance laws the state passed the year before, she pleaded for a waiver of property taxes for the storm victims for one year. She then made an additional pitch for public assistance for the suffering people: "Is it right, is it wise of the nation to force these people into crime by the pangs of starvation?...I feel sure Northern private charity will not hold out, and I do hope you will be able to get government help."[84]

Except for a few gestures, government help was not going to materialize.

[84]Ellen Murray to Governor B. R. Tillman, September 23, 1894, Papers of Governor B. R. Tillman, South Carolina Department of Archives and History.

No "emergency preparedness." Eventually, the governor was moved by the tragic conditions his people faced. He pled not only to the rest of the state but also to the nation for assistance. Calling the storm "unparalleled in its severity," he proclaimed: "What was a prosperous and blooming expanse of rice fields, gardens and farms is today a desert with its very landmarks destroyed, leaving the people without food, without the possibility of getting work or shelter." The governor must have been touched further by the sorrowful handwritten plea of a farmer, a man named Washington Youmans who lived in Hampton County, forty miles from the coast. It was dated September 16, 1893, almost three weeks after the hurricane:

> I now beg leave to address you by letter and let you know that this storm and continued rain afterward has ruined my entire crop. My land was low land in which I cannot make one half crop of cotton. I will not get enough to pay the man that furnished me this year. I also rented corn land and worked to make it. I will not get enough sound corn to pay the rent as three parts are rotten in the field.
>
> I am an old Confederate soldier and always has been a true Democrat, has voted at every election. I has worked hard since the Confederate War, has tried to keep my debts low and all paid.
>
> I am now worse of[f] than I has been since old [Union Gen. Tecumseh] Sherman came through and destroyed all I had [during the Civil War]. My cotton is ruined. My corn is ruined. My rice will not make but little. My potatoes all are rotten in the ground. I have nothing to depend on and is owing something in the neighborhood of $100 hundred and seventy five [sic] dollars. Now I claim that I am in as bad a condition as any in the Lowcountry. The men I owe are coming down on me for the money and when they get [it], I will be left blank. I am now 55 fifty-five [sic] years old. My health bad. I have a wife and seven

children to support. I know I will suffer if I do not get help from some side.

I am, sir, respectfully, fraternally yours.[85]

Or, perhaps the governor was moved by a letter from Dr. William C. Peters of St. Helena Island, who wrote to Dr. James Babcock, the governor's emissary, a week after the storm struck:

I have lost so much with the people that I cannot live unless I can get some remuneration for my services. There's no way of getting any money on this suffering island and although I would be glad to give my service free, I must provide for my family. I have given my services to nearly four hundred sick people and they are increasing daily. Will you do what you can to assist me?[86]

Finally, after it became evident that far greater efforts than those being waged would be required to prevent further fatalities, the governor sought assistance from outside the ruined region. Fortunately, he had heard of the war relief work of the Red Cross organization in other areas of this country and in Europe.

"I am very anxious to know," he said, "if in this calamity it will be of any use to get the Red Cross Society to send its representatives there."[87]

Having read of the disaster from early newspaper stories, Clara Barton, president of the Red Cross, at first believed that the

---

[85]Washington Youmans to Gov. B. R. Tillman, personal correspondence from Varnville SC, September 16, 1893, Papers of Governor B. R. Tillman, South Carolina Department of Archives and History.

[86]William C. Peters to James Babcock, personal correspondence from St. Helena Island SC, September 4, 1893, Papers of Governor B. R. Tillman, SC Archives and History.

[87]Governor B. R. Tillman, correspondence 21 September 1893, papers of Gov. B. R. Tillman, South Carolina Department of Archives and History, Columbia, South Carolina.

inhabitants must all surely have been killed and "there was nothing left to relieve."[88] Thirty years earlier, during the Civil War, she had spent nine months on Union-occupied Hilton Head Island, so she knew the lay of the land and the nature of the people of the Lowcountry. As the daily stories continued in northern newspapers, she then became convinced that "only the state of South Carolina or the general government" could cope with a disaster so enormous.

Nevertheless, when the governor finally called on the Red Cross organization and asked Miss Barton to take over, she responded quickly. Accompanied by the governor and Senator Butler, she traveled to Beaufort in mid-September, three weeks after the hurricane—and discovered a need beyond anything she had imagined.[89]

Where to start? Everything demanded to be done immediately. The people were hungry and ill able to work. There was no work anyway, except the enormous work of cleaning up and rebuilding. There were no shovels and hammers, no nails and lumber, no saws, no carts, and no oxen to pull the carts. There was virtually no money.

The people were sick from drinking from their brackish wells, from going without sleep because of a lack of dry bedding and clothing and shelter, from the bites of the millions of mosquitoes hatched in the standing water, from the bacteria and the stench of rotting carcasses and vegetation. They were dazed, confused, depressed. They needed to be fed and clothed and sheltered. They needed desperately to get food crops into the ground. Even more importantly in the long run, they needed to be reorganized in mind,

---

[88]Clara Barton, *The Red Cross in Peace and War* (American Historical Press, 1903) 201.
[89]Ibid.

spirit, and community so that they could take care of themselves and of one another.

Miss Barton's early investigation found the local relief committees—made up of merchants, bankers, lawyers, all men of prominence and known practical ability—trying hard to meet the desperate needs but weary and overwhelmed. She wrote later:

> They had done and were doing all possible for them to do. With hearts full of pity, hands full of work, themselves large losers by the storm, business nearly wrecked, and needing every remaining energy for the repairing of their own damages and those of the citizens about them.
>
> We viewed the position as a doubtful struggle, which, knowing the financial condition of the country, and the approaching needs of every community for its own, only the fear of a winter famine on these Islands, and the national disgrace which would ensue, if left to chance, or without a firm directing hand among them, gave us the courage to assume the task.[90]

When Clara Barton arrived in the Lowcountry to set up Red Cross headquarters, she found thousands of storm refugees milling about the streets of Beaufort, waiting for the donations of supplies to arrive. "Our first order," she reported later, "was to close every storehouse [of the relief committees], both of food and clothing, and inform the people that all distributions would be hereafter be made from the islands." Her goal was to inaugurate a system—like none ever devised before—that was to restore to active "habits of life a body of utterly homeless and demoralized people, equal in numbers to a small new State."[91]

---

[90]Clara Barton, "Sea Islands," *Lend a Hand* 12 (February 1894): 117.

[91]Clara Barton, *A Story of the Red Cross Glimpses of Field Work* (New York/London: D. Appleton & Company, 1904) 82.

In the beginning of what became the greatest relief field America had ever known, Clara Barton took on the job of feeding 30,000 hurricane survivors with only $30,000 in donated funds for nine months, until spring crops could be harvested. Within a few months, double that number of hungry people would be seeking sustenance—as many as 75,000. Even the savvy, disaster-experienced Clara could not have predicted such a swelling of the numbers. Even in October, however, she knew she needed help.

Appeals denied. South Carolina, she later wrote:

> had no legislature in session until November, when, alarmed for the condition of these people, we directed them to appeal to their state to grant them relief, and in order to awaken the South Carolina General Assembly to a clear sense of its duty, we memorialized that body, explaining the condition of affairs, which full well we felt every man of them knew, and to make the combined appeal still more forcible, the governor sent a special message [in favor of] the relief of the stricken citizens of this proud old state.
>
> Need I tell you that that legislative body, the guardians of the people's weal, at the holidays, adjourned without having made the slightest provision for the relief of these sufferers, if indeed, I might except the fact, that it extended the time of the payment of their taxes one year from date; thus making it possible for the state to collect from them next year what it could not possibly have done this [year].[92]

The US Congress showed itself equally hard-hearted. Through the senator from Massachusetts, a friend of a part-time Beaufort resident, and the support of South Carolina's senior senator, Miss Barton appealed to the federal government:

---

[92]Clara Barton, "Sea Islands," 118.

Ever since the morning after the storm, appeals, petitions, and statements have come from the governor, mayors, councils, and people; the Red Cross has given its statement to the public which, in ordinary times, would have brought in an abundance of funds to meet every possible need; now from all sources there are but $30,000 for this greatest and gravest field of calamity that this country has ever been called upon to care for.

Six thousand houses will have to be built entire or repaired as necessity demands. We have already purchased 500,000 feet of lumber, the generous lumber merchants and railroad officials making it possible to get this large amount" at low prices. "The people can raft this lumber to their islands; but saws, hatchets, and nails must be had to build the houses.

The soil on these islands is wet and sour, the drains and ditches choked up and useless, and vegetation will thrive in but comparatively few places. The people are living on this damp ground in tents, under sheds and tree limbs, and the [subsequent] storm of the 12th of October that swept over this district found them defenseless, and left them in a more pitiable condition than ever. Malaria in acute form is there; typhoid, typhus, and pneumonia will, in the near future, be epidemic....

The remedy we suggest is this: The sum of $50,000 be entrusted to the Red Cross upon good and sufficient bonds in double the amount named to be used wholly and solely in the employment of labor, in putting the islands in proper sanitary conditions, draining the lands so that crops can be produced and houses built for the people, and vouchers made for every expenditure, and if a balance remain, it shall be returned to the Treasury of the United States.

The Red Cross will undertake to feed and clothe these people from the funds and provisions given by our generous citizens.... Free rations must not be given, as that demoralizes and pauperizes....

We pray your consideration of this memorial, and immediate action by joint resolution, for if relief is delayed, the world will soon ring with the humiliating cry that a famine exists in the United States of America.[93]

Immediately after the request was read in the Senate, the senator from Kansas took to the floor to advocate against Congressional disaster relief:

This matter, Mr. President, is a very serious one from every point of view. Not only is it serious, but it is one that in a much enlarged form will very soon be brought to the attention of Congress from other portions of the country.... There are a great many other people who are in circumstances as destitute as these. The miners in the mining regions, many of the farmers in different portions of the country, and especially in the newer portions, are in the same condition. I have in my hand now a printed dispatch in the New York Press, referring to some of the people in the southwestern counties of my own State, where a similar condition prevails. The same is true in...the manufacturing regions in the Eastern States, in New York City, in Boston, and all over the country, from which appeals are coming to us of the same character.

While I believe that we have no constitutional authority, whatever for using the people's money for such a purpose, yet, if this pressed, I shall ask that the area be enlarged to take in the whole country, and that an appropriation sufficiently large be made to set all the idle men in the United States at work. That is all I wish to say.[94]

---

[93]Congressional Record, 53rd Congress, 3399.

[94]*Congressional Record*, 53rd Congress, First Session: 3397–99.

That was, apparently, all that the senator needed to say to accomplish his objective. In the end, his point of view carried. Congress appropriated nothing for disaster relief. Despite such action on the part of the elected officials, the Defense Department loaned tents to the Red Cross. The Treasury Department assigned two deep-draft cutters to assist in deliveries of supplies to the islands. From the Agriculture Department came seeds for garden vegetables. Doctors from the US Marine Hospital Service assisted briefly. The US Navy provided one boat for the Hilton Head mission.

For the tens of thousands of destitute Americans, many of them without roofs over their heads, nothing more of substance came from their government.

Fortunately, Americans as individuals and through their charities, rallied to the appeals for private donations. They had no idea how massive the relief efforts would need to be—or how long they would have to last.

CHAPTER 7

The Sea Island Relief

Always, Sir, set a high value on spontaneous kindness.
SAMUEL JOHNSON

Before preparing her futile pitches to the South Carolina Legislature and the United States Congress, Clara Barton had scoped out the problems and worked out a plan. She realized quickly, she later wrote, "that the relief coming in from outside would soon diminish, as the excitement should wear away, that the sum in hand was painfully small, that the number of destitute was steadily increasing, that the winter was approaching and they must be carried through in some manner till the next year's crops could grow...."

She concluded that "a fixed system of relief must be adopted, a rigid economy enforced" and that "every person who could do so must be made to work for his food and receive food and raiment only in return for labor." She determined that the relief work could be handled only from "persons who had no interests but these to serve and with the light of all experience that could be called to the task" and that, even then, "a successful result was questionable." However, she said, "There was no question of the fatal result of any other course...."[95]

Fortunately, at the age of seventy-two, with many years of war-zone relief and recovery work behind her, Clara had the skills, the experience, the compassion, and the stamina to take charge.

In two large warehouses in Beaufort, believed to have been located on The Point, on King Street between Hamilton and Pinckney streets, Red Cross staff and volunteers set up headquarters for working and receiving and distributing provisions. Pitching tents inside the building, they also arranged their own living accommodations on the site. Clara Barton's desk was a dry goods box with a homemade drawer, her bed a cot. The volunteers used billiard tables for dining, Manila paper for upholstery.

The relief supplies that materialized out of a steady stream of appeals through Northern newspapers reached Beaufort by train and steamboat. The logistics of distribution were cumbersome. From the railroad depot and from the wharves on Bay Street, horses and oxen brought the barrels and boxes of supplies in small carts to the Red Cross warehouses for sorting and shipping. Some of the provisions could be picked up and delivered by carts on Port Royal Island, but most of the relief materials had to be transported by boat.

Clara Barton's journal tells the story: "We are sending out from one hundred to one hundred and fifty barrels [of clothing] and cases [of other goods] a week.... We should send them out even faster than this, for they are greatly needed, only for the scarcity of suit-

---

[95]Clara Barton, *The Red Cross in Peace and War* (American Historical Press, 1903) 201.

FIG 17. Clara Barton, president of Red Cross, in her 70s,
Source: American Red Cross

FIG 18. Clara Barton's personal quarters in Beaufort, Source: American Red Cross

able boats to navigate the shallow, winding creeks among the Islands. Our Government cutters, with their nine feet draught, can only touch the main points along the coast."

Grits and pork. From the beginning, in order to make what was available go around, rations for the hungry people had to be meager—one peck [eight quarts] of hominy grits and one pound of pork a week for every family of seven persons. Those who worked for the community in the various capacities could earn double that amount of food for their families. Sick people would get small portions of tea or coffee, sugar, and bread.

Three and a half months into the work, Clara Barton recorded in her journal: "It was estimated that thirty thousand people were to be fed, clothed, housed, nursed, and generally cared for through a space of eight months, or until the early crops of 1894. The charge was immense; if we shrank from its grave responsibility; not alone the welfare, the lives of these thousands of human beings would be in our hands." Her compassionate heart broke over the sad condition of each individual to whom she administered. But her mind told her to husband the limited resources carefully, to set up a pattern in which the able-bodied earned their rations—and to drain that soggy, low-lying land so that food crops could be raised.

By January, hard, cold reality struck the Red Cross like a blast of hurricane wind. Clara Barton wrote later:

> Imagine, if you can, our consternation, when after a few weeks, petitions and appeals, delegations and committees, from the mainland of South Carolina, lying back of the Islands, and also swept by the storm, began pouring in upon us from North Carolina to Georgia, until another thirty thousand to thirty-five thousand were knocking, knocking, knocking at our door,

beseeching and imploring us in the most heart-rending tones to save them from starvation, and perishing from the cold.…

Thus it is fair to state that in the place of the thirty thousand we innocently took under our charge, there are seventy thousand to seventy-five thousand, who are at this moment depending upon us for the only help they can hope to gain, as insufficient as it is.[96]

The Hilton Head operation. Dr. John MacDonald——a Boston physician who had been rescued from the grounded steamship City of Savannah—volunteered to work for the Red Cross as a service to some of the people who had endured the same trauma he had endured on the night of the hurricane. Fortunately, the trained nurse he married shortly after arriving in the Lowcountry, Ida Battell of Milwaukee, became a willing partner in his mission. From the Red Cross headquarters they set up on Hilton Head Island, the MacDonalds distributed provisions and supervised recovery work for all of southern Beaufort County, the Bluffton area as well as the islands of Pinckney, Bull, Savage, Daufuskie, and Pine—plus other small, inhabited islands.

The steam launch the US Navy made available to the MacDonalds had such a deep draft it could not go into many of the shallow creeks. The provisions from the Navy for a single week were barely enough to get the operation started. As the weeks wore on, when John MacDonald picked up supplies in Beaufort and returned to Hilton Head, he was "met on every hand with appeals for aid of every description," he wrote in his field report. The hungry included the young, able-bodied, and healthy looking as well as weak,

---

[96]Clara Barton, "Sea Islands," *Lend a Hand* 12, February 1894, n.p.

FIG 19. Red Cross distributing food on Lady's Island, Source: American Red Cross

FIG 20. Red Cross headquarters in Beaufort, Source: Library of Congress

"tottering old uncles and aunties." "Malaria at its worst form…was general amongst the people," he said.

Port Royal Sound, a tidal estuary sometimes calm and sometimes filled with pitching seas and white caps, separated many of the storm's victims from the distribution center in Beaufort. Along with food, clothing, housing, tools, and furniture, boats to make the deliveries to islanders were scarce. Had it not been for Mr. Ben Green, a dependable black Hilton Head Island man with a dependable boat, the Red Cross would have failed its mission in the southern part of the county—and many people surely would have perished.[97]

From John MacDonald's report:

> What a scene of bustle our camp presented every Friday when the supplies came [to Hilton Head]! Thirty or forty carts in line at the landing—the boat arrives—all hands help unload and then load the carts, the number of sacks or boxes in each cart being marked down against the driver, and away they go to the camp, three miles away.
>
> As soon as they arrive, the crowd of waiting recipients hand in their [Red Cross relief] cards, and as they are called in one by one, their bags ready opened, the weekly ration is quickly measured, dropped in, the card returned marked, and away they go. While all this is being done, a flotilla of small boats from the other islands in the district, is at the landing, and as each captain presents his order issued by me, my storekeeper gives him the supply for his island, and away he goes home, to enact the same scene with cards and empty bags and hungry people.…

[97]John MacDonald and Ida MacDonald, "Report of Relief Work South of Broad River," 1, Papers of the Red Cross, Manuscript Division, Library of Congress, Washington, DC.

Houses must be built, lumber and nails measured and distributed [tents being provided for the houseless temporarily].
Those whose houses were not damaged were required to help
others rebuild.

Dr. MacDonald later wrote of "constant anxiety" as he carried
the heavy burdens of his charge.[98]

In keeping with the principle that those who could work had to
work for their food, Dr. MacDonald organized basic ditch-digging
as the labor that would benefit the island community most in the
long run. Unless the flooded lands could be drained, they would
never grow the foods needed. And so the shoveling began, and continued, day after day. By the time the Red Cross left in May 1894,
the storm's survivors had created about thirty-seven miles of new
drainage ditches, two to four feet wide and four to six feet deep. The
MacDonalds came to like the island and its people, and bought
property there and stayed at least a year after their assignment was
over—and were gratified to see vegetable crops thriving again in the
summer of 1895—in the ditch-drained fields. Those ditches still
were a feature of the island's landscape well into the twentieth
century.

Sewing societies. Generous donations of good, used, warm clothing arrived by train and boat, but all for adults. Ida MacDonald's
section of the Red Cross's field report showed her worried about the
children who needed clothes, too. "What was to become of the little waifs of the wind, rain and high tide? Evidently these goods had
to be fashioned into little garments. Bedding, comparatively none,

---

[98]Ibid.

and every few minutes the plea, 'Please, miss, just a little bedding to keep the chilluns warm at night.'"[99]

The Red Cross team needed seamstresses, tailors, scissors and needles and thread and thimbles, and many, many hands to do the alterations. After puzzling for a while over the problem, Clara and her assistants hit on the answer. The men were distributing food and rebuilding. The women would make over the used clothing to fit— and make bedding. Some of the donated money must go to buy blankets and fabric. There must be a systematic work schedule.

In a personal foray to Coosaw Island, Clara called a meeting of women to whom she stated the problem clearly and asked for their guidance."These women," she later wrote, "needed only the proper instruction, encouragement, the way opened for them, the suitable material distributed, and the liberty of action and conscience, with no patronage or politics invading their premises. The system formulated for one society became the system for all."[100]

The scenes must have been picturesque, perhaps even cheerful. Ida MacDonald described the sewing society on Hilton Head:

> When all got steadily to work, one would commence a patter song, the rest would quickly join in, and, to the accompanying rattle of the sewing machine, work and music blended. To hear them sing, one would hardly think they had just passed through a great calamity; but it was the calm that follows the storm—they knew their troubles were over, and they were going to get "kiverin" for the "chilluns." How they worked! In this way, 3,400 garments were repaired and given away in this district, besides shoes, hats, etc.

[99]Clara Barton, *The Red Cross in Peace and War*, 255.
[100]Ibid., 259.

Along with sewing societies, Ida MacDonald also ran a school for island children—with as many as forty a day eventually attending.

Islanders in the MacDonalds' district expressed gratitude by naming infant girls "Clara Barton," and infant boys "Red Cross" and wearing handmade red crosses as insignias on their left arms.[101] Some island residents wore the red crosses as an expression of gratitude.

Dock-building. Herbert Lee Bailey, the Charleston man who had spent the night of the storm on Edisto Island, became the Red Cross agent in charge of operations serving the almost 10,000 residents on the islands of Edisto, Wadmalaw, Kiawah, James, and Johns—between Beaufort and Charleston. After three weeks of training under Clara Barton in Beaufort, he demonstrated the diversity of tasks required to keep people from starving to death and to help them become independent again.

In addition to distributing grits and other groceries and building and mending houses, the islanders in his district like those elsewhere had to dig ditches, alter clothing, plant vegetable seeds, and build fences fashioned to keep the pigs and chickens out of the gardens.

They also had to construct a 110-foot wharf into Bohicket Creek—to provide a landing place in the Rockville community on Wadmalaw Island for the boats that would bring in provisions. Despite the lack of dock-building equipment and the lack of adequate food to eat, they worked with the materials and tools available until the job was done. Once the new facility stood in place and began serving its purpose, Mr. Bailey proudly called it "as unique as

---

[101]John MacDonald and Ida MacDonald, "Report of Relief Work," 8.

'tis substantial, having been built by native workmen with raw materials cut and hewn out of the woods, the piles being driven by a pile-driver of our construction."

Red Cross work demanded flexibility and meticulous record keeping. Mr. Bailey also started a school on Wadmalaw. For 8,109 persons living on the islands of his district that became "wards of the Red Cross," the Red Cross records show of "upwards of 200 packages of clothing [barrels, boxes and cases] given out, besides blankets and comforters with special attention for the sick, old, and helpless." He listed foods distributed: grits, 1,527 bushels; meal, 163 bushels; rice, 672 pounds; wheat flour, 23,980 pounds; bacon, 7,000 pounds. He itemized the packages of seeds distributed—140 bushels of seed for corn, 60 bushels of seed for beans, 75 bushels of seed potatoes, and 30 bushels, plus three crates and three boxes, of pea, tomato, okra, and melon seeds.[102]

In Mr. Bailey's final accounting in June 1894, he recalled the raucous, devastating night of the storm ten months before on Edisto Island and wrote about it. "The memory of the hurricane was so appalling that even as I write…now, a cold shudder comes over me, and all the horrors of that awful time come back."[103]

Medical services. Along with the distribution of food and the rebuilding work came the essential tending of the ill and injured, both in the field and at Red Cross headquarters. Dr. Winfield Egan, a Red Cross veteran, described the situation and the process: "The storm had left the sanitary condition of the islands in a very unhealthy state. Many of the wells refilled with a brackish red-col-

---

[102]Herbert Lee Bailey, Report of Relief Work, Papers of the Red Cross, Manuscript Collection, Library of Congress, 12. "Herbert Lee Bailey, Red Cross field report 1893–1894, Clara Barton Papers, Library of Congress, Washington, DC."]

[103]Ibid.

ored water and there were many cases of illness, two-thirds of which were fever, which, in the healthiest times, exists upon the islands."[104]

The Red Cross physicians ran a clinic and dispensary in the Beaufort area from twelve until two daily, made house calls at night and did surgery all day Sundays.

> The average number of patients treated daily between November 9 and April 2 at this clinic was seventy-three. Nights were devoted to seeing those patients who were unable to leave their beds, and this "out-patient service" was only made possible by the tireless, faithful, and competent nurses who had volunteered... Patients came from all parts of the field, and as there was no hospital, they were placed in families who were on the supply list, and something additional given for the care of the sick.[105]

Thus, one person at a time, for eight months, the Red Cross brought medical service to people who rarely if ever had it before the hurricane—but who desperately needed it afterward.

Home-building. Dr. Julian Hubbell, a Red Cross veteran, having worked in the Michigan fires of 1881 and in the snows of Russia with Clara Barton, supervised the quick but sure construction of shelter for the homeless.

> From among those who could handle tools, building committees were formed whose duty it was to repair and rebuild the houses, first, of widows and the infirm, and afterward, their own. These committees were furnished with nails, lumber, and the necessary hardware; tools were purchased, marked with the insignia and loaned until their work should be finished, when

---

[104]Clara Barton, *The Red Cross in Peace and War*, 228.
[105]Ibid.

they would be returned and another committee would take these same tools and begin work on another plantation.

As an example of what occurred, the report from Port Royal Island shows, "Sandy Brown's House, 12 x 18, Rebuilt….Sibyl Robinson's house, moved 200 feet on hill and blocked up," and so on and so on. "Careful reports of tools borrowed and returned, of work done each week, as the basis of additional food support, encouraged accuracy, system, and responsibility."[106]

When Clara Barton wrote the history of the Red Cross ten years later, she referred to field reports and her own recollections and records. "A million feet of pine lumber was purchased from a leading lumber dealer, shipped down the Combahee River, and delivered at the landings on the islands most convenient to the points needed. Each man received his lumber by order and receipt, and was under obligation to build his own house. The work was all performed by them."

Keenly aware of the short attention span of donors, Miss Barton continued steadily to make public appeals and reports and statements of gratitude. She wrote:

> To this moment our thanks go out to the Agricultural Department at Washington, and the great seed houses of all the North, for the generous donations that served to bring once more into self-sustaining relations this destitute and well disposed people.

> The earliest crop to strive for, beside the [vegetable] gardens, was the Irish potato, which they had never raised [along the coast

---

[106]Ibid., 238.

of South Carolina]. Nine hundred bushels were purchased for planting in February. The difficulty of distributing the potatoes lay in the fact that they would be more likely to find their way into the dinner pot than into the ground. To avoid this the court-yard inside our headquarters was appropriated for the purpose of preparing the potatoes for planting.

Some forty women were hired to come over from the islands and cut potatoes for seed—every "eye" of the potato making a sprout—then distributed to them by the peck, like other seed.

I recall a fine, bright morning in May, when I was told that a woman who had come over from St. Helena in the night, wait-ed at the door to see me. I went to the door to find a tall, bright-looking woman in a clean dress, with a basket on her head, which, after salutation, she lowered and held out to me. There was something over a peck of Early Rose potatoes in the basket—in size from a pigeon's to a pullet's egg.

The grateful woman could wait no longer for the potatoes to grow larger, but had dug these, and had come ten miles over the sea, in the night, to bring them to me as a first offering of food of her own raising.

If the tears fell on the little gift as I looked and remembered, no one will wonder or criticize. The potatoes were cooked for breakfast, and "Susie Jane" was invited to partake.

Departure of the Red Cross. Clara Barton's philosophy on the kind of charity required after the 1893 hurricane is worth under-standing today—in a lot of settings:

If it be desirable to understand when to commence a work of relief, to know if the objects presented are actually such as to be benefited by the assistance which would be rendered, it is no less desirable and indispensable that one knows when to end such relief, in order to avoid, first, the weakening of effort and powers for self-sustenance; second, the encouragement of a tendency to beggary and pauperism, by dependence upon others which should be assumed by the persons themselves.

It has always been the practice of the Red Cross to watch this matter closely and leave a field at the suitable moment when it could do so without injury of unnecessary suffering, thus leaving a wholesome stimulus on the part of the beneficiaries to help not only themselves individually, but each other.[107]

On May 20, 1894, almost nine months after the "big blow" rolled its enormous storm surge over the Sea Islands, the MacDonalds once again issued one month's ration of grits and pork for each family, took down the Red Cross flag and closed the relief work for the Hilton Head district. Herbert Lee Bailey's work from Rockville on Wadmalaw Island lasted from December 1893 until August 1894. Dr. Egan reported in person to the Red Cross board in 1895 that Red Cross work continued in various forms in the region, from headquarters in Beaufort, until September 20, 1894, more than a year after the storm. He and Dr. Hubbell stayed in the area for several weeks after most of the relief operations were finished, concerned as they were that the vegetable crops continued to be tended properly and that the people they had helped continue in the disciplined habits the restoration efforts had nurtured.

The official name of the Red Cross Society's mission to the South Carolina Lowcountry was "Sea Island Relief." However, a handwritten Red Cross document dated June 1, 1894, is titled "Sea Island Relief. Special Issue on Main Land." In it lies the evidence of devastation—and the Red Cross relief work—that extended many

---

[107]Ibid., 268.

dozens of miles into the mainland of the state, as well as on the islands.

The report on the mainland said simply that "5,787 families (40,509) people have received 3,186 pecks of grits; 944 lbs. meat; 1,454 lbs. of flour; 260 bbls [barrels], 98 bundles & 13 large boxes of clothing; 5,191 lbs. nails, 102 pieces of tools and garden seeds." As an aside, on a page dated May 31, 1894. "An issue of 1,200 bushels of grits was made at Tomotley [a Beaufort County plantation] for Main Land people."[108]

Without the continuing, repetitive help of newspapers, the supplies would have run out. Through the stories and Miss Barton's reports from the field, potential donors learned of the need again and again, imagined the misery, and provided what was necessary. As was customary at the time, the newspapers that were asked to help obliged with regular appeals and also published on a daily basis the names of the donors and the nature of the donations as they came in. Although it must have been hard for those who had never seen the Lowcountry, never met its people, never witnessed the destructive powers of such a weather phenomenon, never saw such deprivation, thousands contributed generously. Many who had almost nothing shared with those who had less.

In the end, every morsel of grits, every nail, most of the seeds and all of the money spent on the ten-month operation had been donated by the American people out of their personal resources.

Clara Barton's later advice. In correspondence to her South Carolina Lowcountry friends dated February 26, 1895, from Red Cross headquarters in Washington, Clara Barton offered additional, practical advice to the Sea Islanders:

---

[108]"Sea Island Relief Special Issue on Main Land," Papers of the Red Cross, Manuscript Division, Library of Congress, Washington, DC.

Although the claims upon our time are more than we can meet by working all the day and much of the night, the memory and the interest of our faithful Sea Island friends with whom we worked last year, through the months that followed the great storm, still claim much of our thoughts.

Another planting season is approaching, and we are hoping that your people have been doing the preparatory work of ditching for the raising of good crops....

Get the neighbors to join together and clean out the old ditches....

She then listed the vegetables for early planting and those for planting when the time for frost is past.

The garden should be well fertilized and no weeds or grass allowed to grow....

Every Sea Islander should plant NOW a few FIG CUT-TINGS and a few grape cuttings and such other fruit trees as he may be able to get.

...Enjoin the people to keep out of debt, to "owe no man anything." This course will make the road of honesty and integrity easier and shorten the way to plenty and prosperity.

...I will have copies of this letter sent to other leading Sea Island citizens, thus all will be at work at the same time and all will receive the benefits of your united labors by lessened sickness and increased crops.

May the good Lord bless the efforts of a faithful people is the wish of Your friend, Clara Barton. President of the American Red Cross.

CHAPTER 8

A Long, Tedious Aftermath

No fear can stand up to hunger, no patience can wear it out...
JOSEPH CONRAD

A s compassionate and practical as the Red Cross was, it could not feed, shelter and clothe every survivor.

As a veteran in relief work, Clara Barton recorded her methods of organizing; her system for accounting, distributing, and transporting the supplies; the culture she tried to create in the work of meeting the massive needs. As an educator, Rachel Mather rounded out the reality of that place and time by recalling the looks in the faces and the pleas in the voices of exhausted individuals, some of them on the verge of starvation for many months.

Despite generosity and steadiness on the part of professionals and volunteers, scarcity and deprivation persisted. Even into June 1894, some of the hurricane victims continued to forage and scrounge and beg, still without corn, the staple they used to make hominy, grits, or hoe cake and to feed the livestock.

Although the Red Cross records do not refer to Mrs. Mather as a colleague in the long relief struggle, she apparently had an independent, supplemental operation under way during at least part of the time. Like Miss Barton, she used contacts in the North, especially the newspapers, to appeal for donations again and again.

Winter. By January 1894—four months after the hurricane—the Mather School had given out countless bushels of garden seeds, twenty-five barrels of seed potatoes, several hundred hoes, and twenty-four kegs of nails, along with scores of axes, hatchets, and saws. They were provisions to help the people become self-sustaining again, and yet they could not stave off the hunger. Fortunately, along with the grits and pork that were the basics from the Red Cross, Mrs. Mather also gave away food.

One January morning, she said,

> About eight o-clock…we drove out of the spacious yard of the Mather Industrial School with a wagon load of groceries, clothes, and blankets for the sufferers at Seabrook, ten miles away [on Port Royal Island]. After a long ride in the rain and cold we reach our destination and are met by a gaunt, hungry-eyed crowd, which increases outside the cabin, although the rain still falls and the air is raw and cold.
>
> One poor old creature whose wool [hair] is white as cotton comes tottering forward at the call of her name and as we lay a good warm blanket across her poor old withered arm, put into head handkerchief her supply of groceries, she heaps blessings on us and goes with our words of cheer and encouragement.
>
> Here is a young woman with an infant on each arm. Her house blew down at nine o-clock on that awful night of August twenty-seventh, and she had to fly for her life to a neighbor's who took her in and sheltered her although they expected every

moment to see their home go. Fortunately for all only the chimney blew down.

And so we keep on until all the names are called and everything for Seabrook is distributed.[109]

Early in February, Rachel Mather received a request for help from the mainland area around the Combahee River, rice-growing lands outside of the Red Cross's official relief territory and several hours' travel time from her school. She sent an assistant to determine the needs.

Her scout said upon his return:

> The scenes of privation among the Negroes on the six plantations I visited is something dreadful. These poor people...have been passed over until now. A whole shipload of provisions and clothing is needed for these sufferers who are on the verge of starvation. In many cases the scenes are heartrending, the barest possible protection from the weather, heaps of offensive rags on the floor dignified by the name of bedding and on their attenuated forms are embarrassing paucity of attire. In scores of houses there was no sign of food, and the very look in the poor creatures' eyes was...enough to move the stoniest heart....
>
> The rice planters [of the Combahee River area] themselves were well nigh ruined by the hurricane; thousands of acres of ripe grain all ready for harvesting being totally destroyed in a few hours. Willing as they may be to help these poor people, they are quite unable to do so for it is all they can do to supply their own families with even the necessities of life.
>
> One poor old man comes from his door and says, "See, Massa, that gang ob houses what Jesus pushed ober in de storm,

---

[109]R. C. Mather, *The Storm Swept Coast of South Carolina*, 1894, 38, Historical Collection, Beaufort South Carolina County Library.

in ebery one ob dem, deres from four to eight head ob chillum sar and deys all starvin', sar."

"On one of the relief tours an old uncle was met, and being asked what they had to eat, said, 'Nothin' sar, nothin' but a little grits gruel once a day to keep we stomachs togedder.' A poor woman and her large family of children were crying bitterly, having had no food for two or three days.

"This is no exaggeration of the matter, but plain fac's just as we see them."[110]

Shortly afterward, a delegation representing ninety households from the mainland in Colleton County about twenty-five miles away came to Mrs. Mather with the following appeal: "We the people in meeting assembled do petition you in the name of God to help us to something to eat and wear.... We lost all in the late storm, and will thank you for such assistance as we can get, promising to share it with justness to all."[111]

From the low-lying savannahs between Savannah and Beaufort came similar pleas, as described by one of Rachel Mather's scouts:

> I have never seen so many starving, semi-nude, and destitute people in all my life. In some of the homes or huts where I entered, there was not a spoonful of anything to eat. In one cabin I found a family of eight at dinner. They had nothing save a squirrel that was caught in a trap the previous evening. It was sad indeed to see the children drinking the water in which the squirrel was boiled, without a morsel of bread or hominy....
>
> The ground in some places is prepared, but the people have no seeds and of course nothing to buy with.

[110]Ibid., 41.

[111]Ibid., 45.

They are willing to work whenever there is opportunity. I see they also need farming implements.

The people on many of the low rice plantations have received no aid whatsoever since the cyclone. The people are struggling to work the land but cannot raise a crop unless sustained with nourishing food.[112]

Then came an appeal representing 131 sufferers from Hampton County. Mather School sent a supply of meat and grits.

Whites, Mrs. Mather said, held out a long time before asking for help from her, a woman they called a "nigger teacher." However, by midwinter, they too were so desperate they began to come forward in droves. One hundred five white farmers of the Bluffton district, on the mainland in southern Beaufort County, notified Mrs. Mather of their needs, saying there was not a "single peck of corn" among them all.

She described many of them as "footsore and weary" by the time they reached Beaufort, having walked thirty or forty miles to reach the school in hopes of finding help. One pitiful client asked humbly for anything she could give, saying he had tried to sell his horse and his mule but could not find anybody who could afford to buy them and feed them. He had tried to mortgage "three head of cattle" at the store in Walterboro for ten dollars' worth of provisions but he could not make that deal. He tried to borrow on the cattle from the bank but had been told they were insufficient collateral for the loan.

One very respectable looking farmer replied to Mrs. Mather's questions, "I never begged before. I wouldn't now, only I can't see my children starve."

[112]Ibid., 46–47.

Controversy. The misery exhausted the survivors to the point that complaints became as much a part of the relief scene as the barrels of grits and pork and the used clothing from New York. Among other eruptions, the perception arose among whites that one had to be black in order to be given a peck of grits, that white sufferers were denied assistance. A man Mrs. Mather called "a typical cracker" had this to say to her: "I done hear in Colleton County that you give the niggers lot of good things; they need them bad enough too, but I spose you hasn't any objections to helping us too if we have got a white skin."[113]

There also arose the perception that the Red Cross considered the sufferers in the region behind the islands—the vast mainland along a 150-mile stretch of coastline—ineligible for its assistance. Thomas Martin, a white man from the Bluffton district, a peninsula between two rivers in southern Beaufort County, scolded the Red Cross over the way it had organized the relief in his community. Pointing out that whites were a bigger percentage of the population in the Bluffton area than anywhere else in the disaster area, he created a firestorm over what he perceived as neglect of their needs. In a letter to the *Charleston News and Courier,* he lambasted the Red Cross for appointing blacks, Republicans, "pension drawers," and one "creme de la creme hog thief" in Bluffton as its subcommittee for issuing rations.

"The entire [Bluffton] peninsula is composed of large farms from 1,000 to 3,000 acres, and the poor sufferers are tenants on these farms, and the owners of said farms know every sufferer thereon, and are the proper persons to give information," Mr. Martin wrote. He complained that blacks receiving $12 a month (the

[113]Ibid., 50.

equivalent of $240 in today's currency) from the US Government for Civil War service, and blacks who drove "double buggies" and owned as many as two horses, were getting more from the Red Cross than the 200 poor white farm families whose homes and crops had been ruined.

"No doubt the Red Cross is all its high distinction calls for in the North, and perhaps in other parts of our country," he wrote, "but one thing is certain, and that is that here it is an inflammatory failure."[114]

Red Cross agent Dr. John MacDonald, who was responsible for the Bluffton district, responded immediately to Thomas Martin's accusations, accusing him of distorting the facts and exaggerating the needs. Dr. MacDonald wrote that upon his arrival in Bluffton for the first time, he overheard this remark from one of three white citizens standing on the wharf, "That boat has brought the men belonging to that Cross concern which proposes to feed all these worthless niggers."

"I have on my books," Dr. MacDonald wrote, "the name of every family, their condition and needs; when they need help and not before, the Red Cross will help them."

As for the charges the Red Cross behaved in a certain way because of political leanings or racial preferences, Dr. MacDonald said:

> The Red Cross cares not one iota whether a man is Republican or Democrat or anything else. Republican or Democrat, Methodist or Atheist, black or white, color or religion or politics is no ground on which to base an appeal...If they are

---

[114]Thomas Martin, letter to the editor, *News and Courier* (Charleston SC), November 7, 1893, Papers of the Red Cross, Manuscript Division, Library of Congress, Washington, DC.

hungry, naked, homeless, or in any distress which the Red Cross can alleviate, our mission is to them, our aid is for them...Mr. Martin's spiteful cry of partisanship recoils upon himself, for he evidently wishes to make a political issue out of the trivial of men to measure out a peck of grits to starving people.[115]

Proud but hungry. Whites in the Bluffton area adopted a resolution at a mass meeting on April 26, 1894. After expressing gratitude for donations to the "colored sufferers" in their midst, it pleaded to the Red Cross for help for whites, saying "Unless speedy relief is given there will be terrible suffering amongst them."

How that dispute in the Bluffton area was resolved we do not know. We do know that in the spring, a *Columbia Daily Register* reporter did his own investigation for a story about it.

Destitution exists in this vicinity in its worst form, and starvation will follow if help is not extended. The pride of the Anglo-Saxon race has sustained the people. It has not conquered empty stomachs.

These people cannot get relief from their own efforts until the middle of August, when the corn crop is ready to harvest. Without food for their animals the people cannot make their crops. A grass-fed horse or mule is not capable of working behind a plow more than a few hours each day.... A man can go with hunger bothering him but the beast of burden becomes worthless.

The story said that the "better class" had tried to stave off making an appeal but that it could not be helped. It continued: "The

---

[115]John MacDonald, letter to the editor, *News and Courier*, December 1, 1893, Papers of the Red Cross, Manuscript Division, Library of Congress, Washington, DC.

truth is that the Red Cross has given little to the Negroes of Bluffton, and when the distribution takes place every Saturday, there is a grab for what is on hand. The most needy and those unable to push and scramble get left.

"At every humble house I visited there were unmistakable signs of suffering."

Headlines over that story said: "Cursing the Red Cross! Bitter feeling Against it in Beaufort County. White People Get Little and Have to Go to Negro Committees to Get That. Politics Alleged to be in it."[116]

Once Governor Tillman realized that hunger continued to rap at the door of thousands of his state's white people on into the winter, he had urged South Carolinians from the upstate to help their Lowcountry neighbors. In the spring, when he received the sad letter from Bluffton, he was skeptical at first, suspecting that the problems had been exaggerated. On the basis of the same information from what he called "entirely trustworthy sources" and the "personal inspection of an agent," he later changed his mind. It is possible that the story in the *Columbia Register* influenced him as well.

Saying, "I find that there is absolute want and need of prompt assistance, else there will be extreme suffering and probably starvation," he urged South Carolinians to contribute immediately to "the white residents of Bluffton Township, Beaufort County."

It is possible that the governor's compassion evolved only out of his political concerns. By that time, he had announced his campaign for the US Senate. Nevertheless, the citizens of the little town of

---

[116]"Cursing the Red Cross," *Columbia (SC) Daily Register,* May 25, 1894.

Williston, South Carolina, promptly contributed $5.50 for the sufferers.[117] Other South Carolinians almost certainly pitched in also.

On into the steamy summer days and nights of the Lowcountry, almost a full year after the "big blow," the scarcities and the needs persisted. Rachel Mather recorded that the day of June 26, 1894, was filled with men and women knocking at her gate and her door seeking sustenance. She described them not as a mass of humanity but one at a time.

> Abraham Scott is admitted. I hear his pathetic plea for 175 destitute neighbors who he says have good crops growing; if they can only have food enough to sustain them while they cultivate their fields will have enough to live on by August.
>
> We next admit Richard Harrison, committee representing 71 sufferers; he says these have not a morsel of anything to eat in the house, nothing except a few garden vegetables.... We gave him an order for three sacks of grits or 21 pecks.
>
> Boat loads continued to arrive from Okatie and Bellinger Hill [in southern Beaufort County], each with the same sad story of hunger, sickness, and death, and each dismissed with from three to five sacks of grits.

The wants and woes of 600 people had come to her attention by the end of that day.

There is no doubt that famine would have killed many had not generous donors from outside the region responded repeatedly to the requests from the Red Cross, the Mather School and others with contacts in the North, including almost certainly the Penn School

---

[117] "Give and Give Quickly," *Columbia Daily Register*, n.d.

and individuals. How many gave in the almost year of relief and restoration work we will never know. Small acts and large were required—from individuals and businesses, rich and poor; from church groups and benevolent organizations; and from spontaneous relief societies.

In her booklet, *The Storm Swept Coast of South Carolina*, Mrs. Mather listed some of the philanthropists who made her relief work possible: The Friends Relief Association of Philadelphia; the Hawes School Association of Boston; individuals, including a New York woman; churches; the C. E. [?] Society of Springfield, Massachusetts; Unitarian, Quaker, and Baptist groups. The donations came in as large as $150 at a time and as small as $1. The cash totaled about $5,000, the blankets, provisions, tools, nails, and garden seeds another $5,000.

Grateful to them all, she wrote: "May the Lord reward the contributors of these supplies with a hundredfold more in this life, and in the world to come life everlasting."[118]

A legend based on facts. The disaster had been not a one-night stand but a nearly yearlong catastrophe. To help the Lowcountry dwellers cope with it, a St. Helena Island minister wrote a ballad about what his congregation experienced on the night of the hurricane. It so captured the spirit of the people of the time that it became a part of Beaufort County's folklore, sung by old-timers well into the twentieth century. Rivers Varn, well known as a bass soloist in St. Helena's Episcopal Church in Beaufort and as the county's treasurer for almost forty years, recorded the song in the hopes of preserving it for future generations.

---

[118] Mather, 95.

The Storm of 1893

'Twas the twenty-seventh of August
In eighteen and ninety-three
The wind from the north did blowing
The people beginning to fear.

Oh the wind did blow so high
And de storm was all abroad
But yet we recognize in it
The wonderful power of God.

Was the mid-day of Sunday
The wind from the north did blow
The cyclone did come to rage us.
The people beginning to pray.

Oh the wind did blow so high
And de storm was all abroad
But yet we recognize in it
The wonderful power of God.

Have been four hundred bodies
Have been washed ashore
The islands surrounded with sufferers
So God knows how many more.

Oh the wind did blow so high
And de storm was all abroad
But yet we recognize in it
The wonderful power of God.

Now we come to persuade you
Persuade you to come to Christ.
Cast all your sins upon him.
You'll have everlasting life.

Oh the wind did blow so high
And de storm was all abroad
But yet we recognize in it
The wonderful power of God.

Although the haunting song spoke with strength, it revealed only one chapter in a tragic saga. The violent drownings on St. Helena represented the beginning of their troubles. By the time the tallying and estimating were over, it was clear that the hurricane had killed not 400 but about 2,000 Lowcountry residents—and more, perhaps many more, counting those who died in the aftermath. For 30,000 it had wrecked homes, food supplies and the means of earning a living. It put another 40,000 onto the ragged edge of existence for almost a year.

The thousands of survivors suffered and faltered, but most of them survived under conditions worse than anyone could have imagined. The thousands of donors who provided cash and provisions grew weary, but their generosity lasted as long as it was needed. Untold numbers of spontaneous relief organizers, black and white, had to solve a maze of unwieldy problems, and yet they soldiered on day after day, sheltering the homeless, clothing the naked, and feeding the hungry for as long as necessary.

One woman, Clara Barton, deserves the gratitude of the nation for the recovery achievement. Familiar with the nature of the land and its people because of a stint on Hilton Head Island during the

Civil War, she at first thought from reading newspapers about the hurricane that there could be nothing left in the region, and she almost certainly did not relish the thought of relocating to the scene of devastation in isolated coastal South Carolina. Once she responded to the governor's request and came to look first hand, however, she took charge, launched a plan, and followed it through with skill and devotion for nine hard months.

At the age of seventy-two, in a vast terrain of islands and peninsulas, with virtually no government help, during a nationwide depression, Clara Barton organized and led the work that saved tens of thousands of shattered lives and rebuilt the community. The Red Cross projects included nursing the sick and injured and negotiating for building materials. They included helping the storm victims help themselves by digging ditches to drain their water-logged soil, constructing new cabin homes, barns, and fences, and planting potatoes and other vegetables. They included delivering the grits and pork rations over and over until the people could take care of themselves once again. To those who were thus rescued from famine, Clara Barton was a heroine. It is hard to imagine what would have happened if she had not had the compassion, the experience, and the energy to handle the job. Perhaps one day her role will be recognized and honored appropriately, publicly and permanently.

The facts of the hurricane itself were awesome and awful, and the memories and the legends attached to the impacts on the people grew in importance over time. Those who lived through it dealt with its impacts for the rest of their lives—and passed their individual family's hurricane stories on down to their children, who passed them down to their children and so on. Well into the twentieth century, mainland folk who lived in the lowlands near the Combahee

River north of Beaufort held vigils in their praise houses and churches every August, beseeching God to enfold them in his arms and protect them forevermore against such a storm.

Other storms have wrecked the area since 1893, and they also have caused some fatalities. There was a brush by an 1898 hurricane. The 1911 hurricane flooded the Lowcountry's lowest lands and battered boats, roofs and windows. In 1940, a boisterous hurricane with an 8-foot storm surge tore up causeways, docks and bridges; unroofed homes and ripped trees apart. In 1954, Hurricane Hazel and in 1959, Hurricane Gracie beat up the South Carolina coast again. In 1989 Hurricane Hugo terrified thousands in both of the Carolinas as it damaged $7 billion worth of property and snatched off the tops of 1,000,000 pine trees in the Francis Marion National Forest. In 1999 Hurricane Floyd forced coastal residents of South Carolina and Georgia and the east coast of Florida into an enormous, expensive, confusing, hazardous, evacuation before swamping and wrecking eastern North Carolina.

Still, it is the Great Sea Island Storm of 1893 that haunts coastal South Carolinians who know what happened. The St. Helena minister's ballad hints at the horror:

> The cyclone did come to rage us
> Bodies have been washed ashore
> The islands surrounded with sufferers
> So God knows how many more.

About the Authors

Bill Marscher, a retired engineer, and Fran Marscher, a retired journalist, are natives and residents of Beaufort County, South Carolina.

Bill discovered newspaper clippings on the Great Sea Island Storm when he was a young boy and has collected information about it for more than 50 years. Educated at Clemson University and the Massachusetts Institute of Technology, he worked for General Electric and for MIT on the Apollo moon program before returning to the South Carolina Lowcountry in 1969. He has been in business and in public office.

Educated at the University of South Carolina, Fran was formerly a teacher and a reporter, and for 10 years was editor of Hilton Head Island's daily newspaper, *The Island Packet*.

The Marschers tend their vegetable and herb garden and participate in a Great Books Discussion Group. They watch birds, sunsets, and moon rises over the usually calm waters in front of their home on the edge of Mackays Creek near Bluffton.

All together, they have four children and six grandchildren.

Bibliography

Alexander, Edward Porter. South Island Log, 1835–1910. Manuscripts Department, Wilson Library, University of North Carolina, Chapel Hill, North Carolina.

"Appeal of the Sea Island Relief Committee." Clara Barton papers, Manuscripts Division, Library of Congress, Washington, DC.

Bailey, Herbert Lee. Field report from Red Cross agent,. Manuscripts Division, Library of Congress, Washington, DC.

Barton, Clara. *The Red Cross in Peace and War*. American Historical Press, 1903.

———. "Sea Islands." *Lend a Hand* 12 (February 1894): 117–22.

———. *A Story of the Red Cross: Glimpses of Field Work*. New York: D. Appleton and Company, 1928.

Barton, William E. *The Life of Clara Barton*. New York: AMS Press, n.d.

Burn, C. Mabel. "A Certified Correct Experience of Both Storms," November 3, 1959. Quoted in Beaufort County Historical Society Paper #50, The Storm of 1893, attributed to Mr. And Mrs. W. O. Wall, no date. South Carolina Room, Manuscript Collection, Beaufort Public Library, Beaufort, SC.

Chazal, Philip E. *A Sketch of the South Carolina Phosphate Industry*. Charleston: Lucas-Richardson Lithography and Printing Co., 1904.

Christensen, Neils. Diary, Christensen family papers. South Caroliniana Library, University of South Carolina, Columbia.

"Cursing the Red Cross." *Columbia* (SC) *Daily Register*, May 25, 1894.

Congressional Record. November 2, 1893. Washington, DC.

Cyclones of the Carolina Coast, 1893. Charleston Earthquakes and Cyclones, a collection of clippings and pictures, compiled by William Courtenay. Charleston Public Library, Charleston.

Dunn, Gordon E. and Banner I. Miller. *Atlantic Hurricanes*. Baton Rouge: Louisiana State University Press, 1960.

Edgar, Walter. *South Carolina A History*. Columbia: University of South Carolina Press, 1998.

Egan, E. Winfield. Field report from Red Cross physician, Clara Barton papers. No date. Manuscripts Division, Library of Congress, Washington, DC.

Epler, Percy H. *The Life of Clara Barton.* New York: The MacMillan Company, 1953.

The (Washington, DC) *Evening Star,* December 14, 1893. Story credited to *Journal and Courier,* Little Falls NY, November 28, 1893. Clara Barton papers, manuscript, diary, Library of Congress.

Fripp, C. E. Correspondence in family papers. South Caroliniana Library, University of South Carolina, Columbia.

Fripp, Elise. Diary, family papers. South Caroliniana Library, University of South Carolina, Columbia.

Gordon, Asa. *Sketches of Negro Life and History in South Carolina.* Columbia: University of South Carolina Press, 1929.

Grimball family papers. Manuscript Department, Wilson Library, University of North Carolina library, Chapel Hill, NC.

Harris, Joel Chandler. "The Sea Island Hurricanes." *Scribner's Magazine* (February and March 1894): South Carolina Room, Beaufort Branch, Beaufort County Library System, Beaufort, SC.

"A History of Storms on the South Carolina Coast." South Carolina Sea Grant Consortium, 1983. Charleston, SC.

Holmgren, Virginia C. *Hilton Head: A Sea Island Chronicle.* Hilton Head Island SC: Hilton Head Island Publishing Co., 1959.

Johnson, Guy B., *Folk Culture on St. Helena Island, South Carolina.* Chapel Hill: University of North Carolina, 1930; rpt: Folklore Associates, 1968..

Jordan, Laylon Wayne with Robert Dukes Jr. and Ted Rosengarten. *A History of Storms on the South Carolina Coast,* a technical paper, South Carolina Sea Grant Consortium, n.d., Charleston, SC.

Larson, Erik. *Isaac's Storm: A Man, A Time and the Deadliest Hurricane in History.* New York: Crown Publishers, 1999.

Lewis, E. Rhett. "Yachting Experiences in a Cyclone." Family papers of John and William Bowen, given personally to Bill Marscher by William Bowen of Hilton Head Island, SC.

Ludlum, David. *Early American Hurricanes, 1492–1870.* American Meteorological Society.

Martin, Thomas. Typewritten copy of letter to the editor, *News and Courier,* Charleston, SC, November 7, 1893, Clara Barton Papers. Manuscripts Division, Library of Congress, Washington, DC.

Mason, Herbert Molloy, Jr. *Death from the Sea: The Galveston Hurricane of 1900.* New York: The Dial Press, 1972.

Mather, R. C. *The Storm Swept Coast of South Carolina,* Beaufort, SC 1894 publisher unavailable, Beaufort County Library System, Beaufort.

McDonald, John. Field reports from Red Cross agent, Clara Barton Papers. Manuscripts Division, Library of Congress, Washington, DC.

The (Savannah GA) *Morning News*, August 29, 1893–August 31, 1893. A compilation in 1963 Remer Lane, Georgia History and Genealogy Department, Kay Cole Roam, Bull Street Library, Live Oaks Public Libraries, Savannah, Georgia.

News and Courier (Charleston SC), August 29, 1893–September 3, 1893.

New York Herald, September 3, 1893.

The New York World, October 19, 1893.

Oliphant, Mary C. Simms. *The History of South Carolina.* River Forest IL/Summit NJ/ Palo Alto CA/Dallas TX/Atlanta GA: Laidlaw Brothers, 1964.

Penn Community Center Archives. St. Helena Island, SC.

Peters, William C. Letter to James Babcock. Papers of Governor Benjamin R. Billman. South Carolina Archives and History, Columbia, SC.

Pryor, Elizabeth Brown. *Clara Barton Professional Angel.* University of Pennsylvania Press, 1987.

Report from the National Weather Bureau. *Monthly Weather Review* 21/8 (August 1893): Boston, MA.

Rodgers, S. H., quoted in Beaufort County Historical Society Paper #50, Sea Storm of 1893, attributed to Mr. And Mrs. W. O. Wall, n.d. South Carolina Room, Beaufort Branch, Beaufort County Library System, Beaufort, SC.

Rose, Willie Lee. *Rehearsal for Reconstruction The Port Royal Experiment.* New York: Oxford University Press, 1964.

Ross, Ishbel. *Angel of the Battlefield, The Life of Clara Barton.* New York: Harper & Brothers Publishers, 1956.

South Carolina General Assembly. Board of Phosphate Commission. *Third Annual Report to the General Assembly of the State of South Carolina*, Columbia, 1893.

Stovall, Pleasant A. "The Cyclone in the South." *Harper's Weekly* 32 (September 16, 1893).

Tillman, B. R. Papers of Governor Benjamin R. Tillman. South Carolina Archives and History, Columbia, SC.

Wallace, Duncan. *South Carolina A Short History.* Columbia: University of South Carolina Press, 1951.

Workman, W. S. Letter, September 2, 1893, from 154 1/2 St., Manuscripts Collection, Live Oaks Public Libraries, Bull Street Library, Savannah, GA.

Yearbook, City of Charleston, 1893. Charleston: Walker, Evans and Cogswell Co.

Youmans, Washington. Letter to Dr. James Babcock. Papers of Governor Benjamin R. Tillman. South Carolina Archives and History, Columbia, SC.

Index